What people are saying about …

GOD'S FAVORITE PLACE ON EARTH

"In Frank Viola's hands, the story of Lazarus—like Lazarus himself—once again comes to life. In a world where hope is battered and life can so easily beat down the human spirit, we are reminded once more of the possibility of becoming a host of Life."

John Ortberg, pastor and author of *Who Is This Man?*

"*God's Favorite Place on Earth* realigned my heart toward Jesus and His mysterious, confounding, surprising, beautiful ways. It's not often I learn something new when reading a book, but Frank Viola's sharp storytelling and insightful interpretation made me hunger for more of the real Jesus."

Mary DeMuth, author of *Everything: What You Give*

"*God's Favorite Place on Earth* is the kind of book I've discovered I need to periodically find and read. Frank Viola's pen and voice are consistently both penetrating and trustworthy. Beyond his invitingly beautiful writing skill—which makes reading a joy and a sight-seeing tour that brings God's Word into 3-D when he relates narrative passages—I'm grateful for the depth of his themes."

Pastor Jack Hayford, chancellor of The
King's University in Los Angeles

"This is a masterfully engaging book that distills the vision of the Christian life into one focused quest: to be God's favorite place on earth today. I recommend this little volume to all Christians and Christian leaders."

Mark Batterson, *New York Times*
bestselling author of *The Circle Maker*

"Combining masterful storytelling, historical knowledge, biblical insight, and practical wisdom, Frank artfully uses the Gospels' depiction of Lazarus and the small town of Bethany to lay out a beautiful and compelling vision of a God who longs to make every human heart and every church 'His favorite place.' This is a beautifully written, timely, prophetic work all would benefit from reading!"

Greg Boyd, pastor and author
of *Benefit of the Doubt*

"A lot of people write books. Frank writes stories, and in this one we once again see why he's such a master. I'm honored to call him a friend and excited to call him an author I love to read."

Jon Acuff, bestselling author of *Start, Quitter,* and *Stuff Christians Like*

"Frank Viola surpasses himself in his best book yet—a work of serene, soaring magnificence. Part novel, part biography, part theology, part Bible study, Frank's imaginative touch and command of prose haiku leaves the reader resolved more than ever to be a Bethany—God's favorite place on earth."

Leonard Sweet, Drew University, George Fox University, sermons.com

"As I read *God's Favorite Place on Earth* by Frank Viola, my soul began to burn from chapter one. To delve into Lazarus' heart and thoughts … I received a beautiful glimpse into the life of Christ on earth. Lazarus' stories make a perfect foundation for God's truth, God's intimacy. I can't wait to share this book!"

Tricia Goyer, *USA Today* bestselling author of thirty-five books

"In spite of my PhD in Theology, I had never considered the importance of Bethany in the life of Jesus."

Phil Cooke, media consultant and author of *Unique*

"This book exudes love for Jesus. Its creative format offers an inviting window for valuable meditations on what we can learn about the Lord and our relationship with Him from His life and that of some of His closest friends."

Craig Keener, professor of New
Testament at Asbury Seminary

"Reading *God's Favorite Place on Earth* illuminates the story of Jesus in such a new and captivating way that it's bound to impact your life. Read this powerful book and reconnect with the Lord's heart for every Christian, every church, and every city."

Pete Wilson, pastor and author of
Plan B and *Empty Promises*

"*God's Favorite Place on Earth* is engaging fiction, poetry, theology, and devotion all put under one cover."

Anne Marie Miller, author of *Mad Church
Disease* and *Permission to Speak Freely*

"With a mix of creative narrative and pastoral insight, Viola reveals what these friends of Jesus meant to Him—and what that means for us."

Joe Carter, editor at The Gospel
Coalition and The Action Institute

**READ MORE ENDORSEMENTS BY OVER FORTY-FIVE
AUTHORS AT GODSFAVORITEPLACE.COM**

GOD'S FAVORITE PLACE ON EARTH

FRANK VIOLA

David C Cook®
transforming lives together

GOD'S FAVORITE PLACE ON EARTH
Published by David C Cook
4050 Lee Vance View
Colorado Springs, CO 80918 U.S.A.

David C Cook Distribution Canada
55 Woodslee Avenue, Paris, Ontario, Canada N3L 3E5

David C Cook U.K., Kingsway Communications
Eastbourne, East Sussex BN23 6NT, England

The graphic circle C logo is a registered trademark of David C Cook.

The website addresses recommended throughout this book are offered as a
resource to you. These websites are not intended in any way to be or imply an
endorsement on the part of David C Cook, nor do we vouch for their content.

For Bible credits, see page 206.

LCCN 2013933125
ISBN 978-0-7814-0590-4
eISBN 978-1-4347-0558-7

© 2013 Frank Viola
Published in association with the literary agency of
Daniel Literary Group, Nashville, TN 37215.

The Team: Alex Field, Amy Konyndyk, Nick Lee, Caitlyn Carlson, Karen Athen
Cover Design: Amy Konyndyk
Cover Image: David Roberts, Historical Picture Archive/CORBIS

Printed in the United States of America

First Edition 2013

2 3 4 5 6 7 8 9 10

050613

Narratives anchor people to a unified vision.
May this book give you a unified vision
that will govern the rest of your life.

CONTENTS

INTRODUCING AN AMAZING VILLAGE

In every generation, Christians face the same challenges—namely doubt, discouragement, fear, guilt, division, rejection, and the struggle against consumerism and complacency.

The Gospels narrate the incredible story of Jesus' earthly life. Yet there is a story within this narrative that's often missed. And to my mind, it's the greatest story never told—a narrative within the narrative.

That narrative is the story of Jesus' repeated visits to the little village of Bethany.

When we extract the story of Bethany from the four Gospels and trace the footsteps of our Lord there, a beautiful saga emerges. This saga speaks to the challenges of doubt, discouragement, fear, guilt, division, rejection, consumerism, and spiritual apathy. Challenges we all face as believers.

My object in this book is to tell the story of Bethany and bring its powerful message to life. The reason? *Because that narrative changed my life.* And I'm hopeful that it will change yours also.

This book is a work of biblical narrative. The Gospels give us the meat of the story of Bethany, but I've filled in the details by creating dialogue, action, and atmosphere. These details add color and texture to the story. They transform the story into vivid 3D Technicolor, unearthing uncommon insights from the biblical text.

Note that I've drawn the creative details from first-century history. As such, they are fully consistent with the biblical record and New Testament scholarship.

Even so, this isn't a scholarly work. As a result, different possibilities derived from the biblical data are deliberately left out. My narration is according to what I consider to be the best research available.

According to the Gospels, four main characters lived in Bethany: Martha; her sister, Mary; and their brother, Lazarus. A person named "Simon the leper" also lived there.

Some people may think that Jerusalem is God's favorite place on earth. And in a sense they are correct. Jerusalem is central in the Bible. It is where God put His name and where He chose to presence Himself in the temple.

When Jesus arrived on the scene, however, the holy city of Jerusalem became something that God never intended. And it rejected its Savior. So much so that it crucified Him. The tears of Jesus over Jerusalem, therefore, were not tears of satisfaction and joy. They were tears of sorrow for rejecting its Messiah. In the following pages I will demonstrate that the place where Jesus Christ—God incarnate—was happiest, the most satisfied, and felt most at home was Bethany. It is in this sense that I am using the phrase "favorite place."

In the pages that follow, Lazarus will tell the story in six parts. Following each frame of the story, a "walking it out" section will practically apply some of the crucial points of the narrative that bear on our lives today. The book concludes with a "talking it over" section to help guide discussions for churches and small groups.

As you read the incomparable story of Jesus in Bethany, I expect the profound significance of what our Lord did in this village to come to life for you. And when you are finished, I hope you will discover the meaning of God's favorite place on earth.

FACTS ABOUT BETHANY

• Bethany was a tiny village a little less than two miles (three kilometers) east of Jerusalem. It was located on the southeastern slopes of the Mount of Olives.

• Opposite Bethany was the garden of Gethsemane. Gethsemane, which means "olive press," was located on the western slopes of the Mount of Olives.

• Bethany was full of palm trees, almond trees, olive trees, pomegranate trees, and fig trees. The shade of those trees offered a welcome retreat for tired and wearied travelers.

• During the six days preceding His crucifixion, Jesus visited Jerusalem in the daytime and retreated to Bethany to spend the night. He spent the last six nights of His earthly life in

Bethany, where He found refuge, repose, safety, acceptance, and peace.

• The precise meaning of *Bethany* is unclear. Some believe it means "house of the poor." Others suggest it means "house of the afflicted." Others say it means "house of dates." Still others believe it means "house of figs." In this book, we will use the last definition. You will understand why later.

• Jesus especially loved three people in Bethany: Martha, Mary, and Lazarus. Lazarus and his two sisters were dear to our Lord, likely drawing the warmest feelings from His heart.

> So the sisters sent word to Jesus, "Lord, the one [Lazarus] you love is sick."[1]

> Jesus loved Martha and her sister and Lazarus.[2]

> "Our friend Lazarus has fallen asleep ..."[3]

> Then the Jews said, "See how he loved him [Lazarus]!"[4]

• Some scholars suggest that Mary and Martha were the two most prominent women in Jesus' life after His mother. This is probably accurate.

• The Bethany family (Lazarus, Mary, Martha, and Simon) appears to have been well-off financially. The following features indicate their financial status: the size of Martha's house (the house seated Jesus, His twelve disciples, and others); the type of tomb that was used for Lazarus (similar to the one that belonged to Joseph of Arimathaea[5]); the fact that Lazarus was wrapped in linen (the finest textile then used for shrouds); and the ultra-costly perfume that Mary poured upon Jesus' head and feet.[6] While the family was well-to-do, they didn't appear to be rich. Martha cooked and served, and there is no mention of household servants.

• It appears that Martha was the older sister (her name is often listed first), Mary was the younger sister, and Lazarus was the younger brother. John called Bethany "the town of Mary,"[7] indicating that Mary was the favored daughter of this well-to-do family. The family also had friends, and perhaps relatives, who lived in nearby Jerusalem.[8]

• In the Gospels, Lazarus never speaks, Mary speaks once, and Martha speaks six times. This is probably reflective of their personalities.

• Simon the leper also lived in Bethany.[9] Most scholars believe that Simon was a relative of Martha, Mary, and Lazarus. Some have argued that the most reasonable conclusion is that Simon was the father of Lazarus and his two sisters. They point out that in Luke 10, the home Jesus visited in Bethany is said to belong to Martha. In Mark 14, the home is said to belong to Simon. If Simon was Martha's father, then this would make perfect sense since they shared the same house. This would also allow us to easily reconcile the banquet mentioned in John 12 with the versions given in Matthew 26 and Mark 14. In addition, it would explain why Simon was part of the family's private affairs. So in this book, we will assume that Simon is the widowed father of the family.

All of the above facts will help you to better understand the story that will unfold in the following pages …

Chapter 1

APPRECIATING BETHANY

It's been more than thirty years since I met Him. The day He first entered our home is etched in my mind forever. I shall never forswear those memories.

My sisters, Mary and Martha, are no longer with us. Neither is my father, Simon, whom Jesus healed of leprosy.

Most of the Teacher's close disciples, all of whom I had the privilege of knowing, have rendered their lives for His Name's sake.

A number of them committed to the written page their own encounters with Him. Words that I've read and consider to be God-breathed.

Since I am not sure how much longer I have left on this earth, I wish to leave behind the story of the times Jesus came to my hometown, Bethany, and of all the people He forever changed while He was here.

The One who lived before the earth existed spent only thirty-three years on the planet. And God gave me the unique honor of sharing some of those years with Him.

I did not know it at the time, but the Galilean prophet was rejected everywhere He went. When I discovered this, the irony dawned on me.

Here was the God of the universe, clothed in human flesh, turned down, cast away, refused in nearly every quarter in which He stepped.

The Creator was rejected by His own creation.

When He was born, Bethlehem closed its doors to Him. So He came into the world in the place where animals were fed.

Luke always had an eye for detail. In his recent narrative about the Savior, he wrote,

> And she gave birth to her first child, a son. She wrapped him snugly in strips of cloths and laid him in a manger, because there was no lodging available for them.[1]

But that's not all. When He was two years old the government hunted Him down like an animal. Consider it. The

Son of God—a mere child—treated like a dangerous creature unworthy of breath. Matthew recounted the sad ordeal:

> When Herod realized that he had been outwitted by the Magi, he was furious, and he gave orders to kill all the boys in Bethlehem and its vicinity who were two years old and under, in accordance with the time he had learned from the Magi.[2]

When He began His public ministry, He was rejected by His own people—*my people*—the Jews.

John set it forth this way in his account:

> He came to that which was his own, but his own did not receive him.[3]

Jesus was despised, rejected, and belittled by the Jewish elite who dominated Jerusalem. They eventually colluded with the Romans and put Him to death. Yet with gripping pain and sorrow, He still loved the city that betrayed Him. Matthew rehearsed His prayer in his narrative:

> O Jerusalem, Jerusalem, you who kill the prophets and stone those sent to you, how often I have longed to gather

your children together, as a hen gathers her chicks under her wings, but you were not willing.[4]

When He sought entrance into the despised region of Samaria, the Samaritans rejected Him also. Luke told the story, saying,

And he sent messengers on ahead, who went into a Samaritan village to get things ready for him; but the people there did not welcome him, because he was heading for Jerusalem.[5]

He was even rejected by His own hometown, Nazareth, the place where He grew up. Mark captured the scene in his gospel:

"Isn't this the carpenter? Isn't this Mary's son and the brother of James, Joseph, Judas and Simon? Aren't his sisters here with us?" And they took offense at him.

Jesus said to them, "Only in his hometown, among his relatives and in his own house is a prophet without honor."[6]

Here was the earth's Creator. The One who made all things and for whom all things were made … unwelcomed by the very world that came from His hand.

I'm reduced to tears every time I think about it; there was only one exception to this widespread rejection.

Throughout His short time on earth, my sisters and I determined that there would be one place where Jesus of Nazareth, the Christ of God, would be welcomed.

A little village called Bethany.

My hometown.

God's favorite place on earth.

Let me tell you the story …

THE SACRED TEXT

Foxes have holes and birds of the air have nests, but the Son of Man has no place to lay his head.

—Luke 9:58

WALKING IT OUT

Not the crushing of those idols,
With its bitter void and smart;
But the beaming of His beauty,
The unveiling of His heart.

Ever since He stepped onto this earth as a human being, the Lord Jesus Christ—God in human form—was rejected.

The only exception was Bethany.

Regrettably, history has repeated itself ever since Christ ascended into heaven. He is still rejected by much of the world.

More disheartening, He is often rejected by His own people, contrary to their knowledge or intentions.

If you are a Christian, you too will face rejection. You will face it from those who don't know the Lord and who are hostile to His ways.

> In fact, everyone who wants to live a godly life in Christ Jesus will be persecuted.[7]

But the rejection that cuts the deepest is that betrayal which is inflicted by your fellow brothers and sisters in Christ.

If you choose to follow the Lord seriously, you will face rejection from some of God's people.

The rejection of Jesus was foreshadowed in our Lord's own life.

∾⌇∽

In the days of His flesh, Jesus wasn't just rejected by the Romans and the Samaritans; He was also rejected by His own people, the Jews. And that last rejection brought tears to His eyes.[8]

In fact, it was *that* rejection that got Him killed.[9]

Our Lord was wounded in the house of His friends.[10]

Even one of His own disciples who walked with Him for three years betrayed Him into the hands of sinners.[11]

Yes, dear Christian, if you follow the Lord Jesus utterly, you too will face rejection from some of your fellow Christians. This has been the testimony of every servant of God. And Jesus promised as much:

> No servant is greater than his master. If they perse-
> cuted me, they will persecute you also....[12]

To be rejected by a fellow believer is a painful experience. But keeping four things in mind when it happens will help. Those four things are:

(1) Remember that you are entering into the Lord's own sufferings

> I want to know Christ and the power of his resurrection and the fellowship of sharing in his sufferings, becoming like him in his death.[13]

> For just as the sufferings of Christ flow over into our lives, so also through Christ our comfort overflows.[14]

God allows rejection to come into our lives so that we may have the painful privilege of sharing in the fellowship of Christ's sufferings. Through such sufferings, we understand more about our Lord and how He felt in His own afflictions.

Rejection from fellow Christians is part of that fellowship.

The Christian life is a reliving of the life of Jesus. So your destiny is His experience.

While we don't experience His deity or His atoning sacrifice (both of which are unique to Him), we do enter into His sufferings, His death, His resurrection, and His ascension to heaven.

The Christian life holds for you all that it held for Christ.

(2) Remember that Jesus Christ understands the agony of being rejected because He experienced it Himself

When you touch the pain of rejection, Jesus sympathizes with you.

> For we do not have a high priest who is unable to sympathize with our weaknesses, but we have one who has been tempted in every way, just as we are—yet was without sin.[15]

The Lord is able to comfort you because He knows exactly what you're going through. He understands your pain, having been there Himself. So we can rest our heads on a God who knows what it feels like firsthand. And He—*the God of compassion*—comforts us in such suffering.[16]

(3) Rejection is designed by God to bring brokenness into your life so that you may minister more effectively

We live in a day where the popular idea behind ministry training is to focus on developing one's gifts. Gift inventories, personality surveys, and strength indicator tests are the rage among those who want to be equipped for ministry today.

But these kinds of tests set your eyes on *your* gifts. They put the focus on *your* strengths and *your* natural abilities. They make *you* the center of attention.

However, the Lord is far more interested in your weaknesses than in your strengths. He's interested in breaking you. Why? Because when there is less of you in the way, there is more room for Him to work.

> Apart from me you can do nothing.[17]

It's so easy to buy into the me-centered ministry culture today—the building up of one's self-esteem by focusing on human goodness. But God's goodness, and not ours, is the basis for our worth.

After talking at length about his sufferings and weaknesses, Paul made this surprising statement:

> But he said to me, "My grace is sufficient for you, for my power is made perfect in weakness." Therefore I will boast all the more gladly about my weaknesses, so that Christ's power may rest on me. That is why, for Christ's sake, I delight in weaknesses, in insults, in hardships, in persecutions, in difficulties. For when I am weak, then I am strong.[18]

God's idea of ministry training is a broken vessel. His idea of spiritual preparation is suffering, which includes rejection.

Here is the biblical recipe for ministry preparation—a recipe that's glaringly absent from the pages of most ministry training manuals today:

> For we who are alive are always being given over to death for Jesus' sake, so that his life may be revealed in our mortal body. So then, death is at work in us, but life is at work in you.[19]

Criticism and rejection are God's tools for liberating His servants from human control and the desire to please men.

To make you a useful vessel in His hands—"fit for the Master's use"—God will sovereignly bring rejection into your life. Jacob is not alone in encountering an angel who will break his natural strength and leave him with a limp.

The crippling touch of God still disables those who rely on their own gifts and talents.

While modern ministry training is aimed at developing your natural abilities, leadership skills, independence, and self-confidence, God wants you to rely on Him instead of yourself. Why? So that any power you utilize may be completely of Him. And in so doing, you will discover the secret of being weak so that He may be strong.

> But we have this treasure in jars of clay to show that this
> all-surpassing power is from God and not from us.[20]

As we survey church history, we discover that A. W. Tozer's piercing observation is most accurate: "All great Christians have been wounded souls."

Indeed, God breaks us to build us. And the more naturally gifted a person is, the more breaking is required. So from God's standpoint, it's a privilege to be among the walking wounded.

While brokenness is difficult, it's beautiful because it makes God look good. Your natural gifts draw attention to yourself while brokenness draws attention to your Lord. With this in mind, power is dangerous in the hands of an unbroken vessel.

Hemingway fittingly said, "The world breaks everyone and afterward many are strong at the broken places." The Christian understands that God is the One who breaks us, and He uses the world as His instrument for doing so.

This brings us to the subject of loss. From childhood, we are all taught how to win. We're taught how to gain advantage and get our own way. Yet the secret of fruitful ministry is in learning how to lose.

When we're always winning and getting our way, Jesus Christ isn't getting His way. So the way to gain with God is to lay down our lives and lose.

> Then Jesus said to his disciples, "If anyone would come
> after me, he must deny himself and take up his cross
> and follow me. For whoever wants to save his life will
> lose it, but whoever loses his life for me will find it ..."[21]

Jesus talked a lot about losing, taking up our cross, denying ourselves, and laying down our lives.[22] These are the fruits of brokenness before God.

It's not hard to spot a Christian in ministry who isn't broken. Unbroken people don't know how to lay their lives down and lose. They only know how to try to win.

If they're criticized, they retaliate. If they're attacked, they return fire. If misunderstood, they defend in anger. They are capable of doing all sorts of damage to others in order to save their own ministries and keep their reputations.

On the contrary, people who have been broken by the hand of God know how to turn the other cheek. They know how to go the second mile. They know how to give their coats when asked for their shirts. They know how to speak well of those who misrepresent them. They know how to return good for evil. They know how to lose. And in so doing, they exhibit the Spirit of the Lamb and allow God to win.

In the words of E. Stanley Jones, "The God I find in Christ is a God who overcomes evil with good, hate by love, and the world by a cross."

Again, it is through the wounding and the breaking we experience that the life of Christ can be released through us. And that is where the secret of fruit bearing lies. So don't nurse your wounds. Let them turn to gold and not hyssop.

(4) Remember Christ's reaction to the people who rejected Him

There are two ways to respond to rejection. One is to react in the flesh and become bitter and angry and to retaliate against those who have hurt us. The other is to react in the Spirit, which is the way Jesus responded to those who rejected Him.

> To this you were called, because Christ suffered for you, leaving you an example, that you should follow in his steps. "He committed no sin, and no deceit was found in his mouth." When they hurled their insults at him, he did not retaliate; when he suffered, he made no threats. Instead, he entrusted himself to him who judges justly.[23]

Jesus Christ refused to allow bitterness to take root in His heart. After standing under a hail of criticism from the Jews, the Lord stood before Pilate and was silent. When the Romans pierced His hands with six-inch nails, He prayed that God would forgive them. And when He rose again from the dead, He wasn't spewing venom over those who crucified Him.

Jesus didn't seek vengeance against those who misunderstood Him, nor did He justify Himself, setting the record straight in light of the lies that were told about Him.

While the death of Jesus is immortal, the unjust and indescribable pain that He suffered at the hands of sinful men was not upon His lips when He broke free from the grave.

No, He was utterly silent about the entire ordeal. He acted as though it never happened.

> Forgetting what is behind and straining toward what is ahead.[24]

Many Christians cannot get over rejection, let alone misunderstanding. And that is why there is no resurrection in their lives.

In our own natural power, we are incapable of responding to pain the way Jesus did. But the good news of the gospel is that He lives inside of us, giving us both the power and the will to do His good pleasure.[25]

The secret is in letting go.

Chesterton rightly said, "One sees great things from the valley; only small things from the peak."

A disciple in the school of Christ often learns more by suffering than by studying. Spiritual growth picks up its pace whenever you're looking down from a cross, and brokenness is a prerequisite for usefulness.

If you are a Christian, then, expect to follow in the footsteps of your Lord. You will know the scalding pain and heartbreaking disillusionment of rejection.

How you respond, however, will determine if you become broken or bitter.

If you view such things from a natural plane, you may get so depressed that your eyes cross, feeling that you have to climb up just to reach the bottom. These are the typical emotions that provoke grudges.

Someone once said that you don't hold a grudge. It holds you. Holding a grudge is self-inflicted pain. Consequently, bitterness doesn't imprison those who hurt you. It imprisons you.

Again, we do not have the strength to forgive others who wound us. But we have One who indwells us whose name is Forgiveness. And He is able and willing to forgive *through* us, releasing us and others.

You'd be wise, therefore, to seek to get behind the eyes of our Lord and see things from His vantage point.

You have a God who knows what it feels like to be rejected. But He also knows the preciousness of having a Bethany. A place where He is completely received, honored, and appreciated.

That is the subject of our next chapter …

Chapter 2

AWED IN BETHANY

My oldest sister, Martha, scurried around the house, her lips pursed together in concentration. She and Mary spent the entire afternoon in the courtyard, preparing a meal for Jesus and His twelve followers.

When Martha was in prep mode, we all walked on pins and needles. She was known to push us out the door if we got in her way.

Martha demanded that the preparations be the best. Especially given the unique honor of hosting the Teacher (as we affectionately called Him). As always, Mary quietly followed her directions.

When she was alive, Martha was the most practical woman I knew. Unable to sit still, she was always busy, alert to detail, a perfectionist at heart. She was a doer, an implementer. She was gutsy, freely speaking whatever was on her mind. Yet few people had a more generous heart.

When my mother died and our father was stricken with leprosy, Martha—the senior member of the family—stepped into the role of caretaker. Because I was only five years old when my mother passed away, I regarded Martha as a mother. She was seven years older than me.

With such responsibility on her shoulders, Martha felt constant pressure. But never once did I see her shrink from her tireless service and trying sacrifice. Many nights her shoulders sagged from the day's work, but she still managed to tell me a story before bed.

Martha's hospitality garnered adoration from the people of Bethany. She would often prepare meals for our neighbors and friends when they were ill.

What I remember most about her were her hands. Calloused and coarsened from years of hard work, they were the hands that fed and comforted me throughout my childhood.

I would often stare at her hands.

Mary was cut from a different mold. She was born two years before me. She was a reflective soul, tender and given to times of solitude. If you walked into a room full of people, you would be hard-pressed to notice her.

None of us ever married. We devoted our lives to helping our father after our mother died. I followed in the footsteps of my father (before he fell sick), plying my trade as a silversmith, melting and twisting metal into useful pieces. And God blessed my work.

∽◌◡◦

Early sunlight filtered through the leaves of the olive tree next to my bedroom window. Jesus and His followers had just left Samaria on their way to Jerusalem.

Despite my father's sickness, which had escalated slowly, he still managed to walk with me into the village to visit a friend. I noticed his lesions were spreading and becoming more painful.

Suddenly, we saw a crowd clustering together. Jesus, the prophet from Galilee, was praying for some people who were sick … all of whom I personally knew.

My father's leprosy had not graduated to the point where he was forced to be quarantined. But it was fast moving in that direction.

We both knew of Jesus and of His teaching. My sisters and I, along with our father, had heard Him teach in Jerusalem at the Passover festival earlier that year.

We found ourselves spellbound by His words. Jesus spoke like no other teacher in Israel. Not once did He quote another rabbi as all the other teachers did. He instead used parables and metaphors and claimed that Almighty God had directly inspired what He said.

Our hearts burned within us as He spoke. Time stood still. Our eyes never moved from His face. The music of His voice, the majesty of His person, and the magnetism of His words ravished our hearts.

There was an air of sovereignty about Him. His confidence felt almost tangible, and it made me stand taller. At the same time, He was gentle and approachable. An unusual combination.

My father almost stumbled over the uneven stones. He gripped my arm, and I held him up. Some of the bandages on his right arm had come off, and his leprosy-marked skin was exposed for all to see. I saw others glance at him, and I felt their disdain.

We saw Jesus approaching ahead. I wanted nothing more than for my father to be healed of his disease.

"Jesus," I called out, "please come here."

My father ducked his head, almost embarrassed that he should be the center of any attention.

Jesus walked over to us and asked, "What would you like Me to do for you?" I'll never forget it. My father said hesitatingly, "I have leprosy. I want to be made whole."

Jesus looked straight at him, put one hand on his forehead and the other on his chest, and boldly said, "You are clean."

My father straightened. Awe filled his face. Jesus motioned for me to come forward and examine him. Immediately I removed the bandages from his arms. The spots and lesions had vanished!

Dumbfounded, I pushed the words past the lump in my throat. "Thank You," I said. After I could speak more, I told Him, "We live in Bethany. If you are able, we would like to prepare a meal for You and Your disciples for dinner."

My father clasped his hands together. "Yes, please, it would be our honor. I have two daughters, and they would be thrilled to have You join us."

Jesus responded, "Thank you. My disciples and I will arrive at the eleventh hour."

Euphoric, I said, "Wonderful!" I gave Him directions to our house.

As we journeyed home, my father began to weep. "I cannot believe what just happened. I was so worried that I would have to leave you and the girls. It was my greatest nightmare."

I couldn't hold back the tears myself.

When we returned home, we told Mary and Martha that Jesus was in the village and about how He had healed our father. They were overjoyed. Tears coursed silently down Mary's cheeks.

Martha examined him from head to toe (his eyes still red from crying). There was no sign of leprosy. The white patches of dead skin were gone, and so was the exposed infection underneath. Our father was completely healed.

I said to Martha, "But that is not all … the Teacher and His disciples are coming here tonight. We invited them for dinner."

"What?" Martha said, stepping back.

"That's wonderful!" Mary said.

"Wonderful?" Martha shot me a look. "I hope you've learned how to cook and clean. We don't have time. A meal for so many?"

Martha crossed her arms over her chest. I knew how much she loved to serve others, despite all her huffing and puffing.

"Tell me what to do," I said.

"Firewood," she barked. "Bring me lots of it."

Mary eased her slender frame past Martha, asking if there was anything she could do to help.

"Of course," Martha snapped. "Get some baskets, we need to go into the city."

Mary brushed her jet-black hair over her shoulder, grinned at me, and turned back to our older sister. "At your service."

Martha began plotting how she was going to feed seventeen people. She had hosted many meals before, but this would be the largest she had ever prepared.

She paced back and forth. Her skirt swishing around her short legs, she began muttering about the project. "We're going to need lots of dates, goat cheese, garlic, dill, bay leaves, coriander, mustard seeds, and lentils. I know exactly what I will prepare for everyone."

Mary and Martha rushed to Jerusalem to obtain what they needed.

∽◦∼

The day passed quickly. A symphony of noise clanged from the courtyard all day. Shadows crisscrossed the road in front of our house. The evening sky heralded Jesus' arrival at the eleventh hour.

Martha greeted Jesus warmly, receiving Him gladly into our home.

We later discovered that the Teacher and His followers had just been rejected in Samaria. What a stark contrast to come to a household that knew who He was and appreciated Him for it, though we would learn so much more about Him in the days to come.

Meeting His twelve followers for the first time was memorable. They were all young men; most were in their late teens.[1]

Matthew had to bend down to get through the doorway. John didn't say much, but he greeted Martha, Mary, my father, and me with a warm hug. He reminded me of Mary. Peter impulsively tried to dictate where everyone sat at the table. He reminded me of Martha. That night, Thomas privately suggested to me that my father should see the village doctor to verify the completeness of his healing. He was a questioner.

The others were pleasant to be around. They were careful observers, studying Jesus at all times.

Then there was the Teacher Himself. He was so confident, yet so warm. He emitted a quiet strength. But He was terribly meek as well. I felt immense love and acceptance from Him.

Jesus and I were the same age—thirty-one when we first met.

Martha escorted them all into the public room. Our home in Bethany is one of the largest in the village, so all of us— *fifteen men*—sat comfortably.

My father and I took our place at the Teacher's feet along with His disciples. Jesus began teaching about the kingdom of God and how to pray.

Mary caught my eye. She was roaming in the courtyard, peeking into the room, stirring a bowl.

Suddenly, she left the courtyard and sat at the Teacher's feet with the rest of us.

My jaw dropped.

Even though I've known Mary to be a person who follows her heart, I never dreamed she would be so bold as to take a place with the men. I scanned the faces of the disciples. No one batted an eye.

My father and I quietly looked at one another in surprise.

Every other teacher would have scolded Mary severely for taking the posture of a disciple and sitting in the public room, where only men were permitted.

But Mary was an instinctive soul. Somehow she knew that Jesus would permit her to sit at His feet with the others, even though it was considered scandalous.

Just ending a sentence, Jesus looked at Mary, faintly smiled, and carried on His teaching.

In reverent and rapt contemplation, Mary sat at the feet of Jesus with the rest of us. She was attentive and attuned. Did her heart soar at hearing His words as mine did? We both took in every word and gesture, gaining the courage to pull in closer.

I could hear the banging of pots in the courtyard. The sound grew louder by the second. I sensed that Martha was upset, and I was right. She stormed into the room with her arms folded. Her voice echoed off the rafters.

"Lord, don't You care that my sister has left me to do all the work by myself? Tell her to help me!" she protested.

I flinched.

An awkward silence filled the room.

Mary, who had been listening to Jesus in sacred worship and silent wonder, dropped her head. She did not utter a word. The disciples froze.

My heart went out to Mary. I felt embarrassed for her. I knew that Martha's words stung. And I was ashamed that Martha brought Jesus into the matter, accusing Him of being careless. A flash of anger crossed my chest.

Jesus turned to Martha and gently but sternly said,

"Martha, Martha. You are worried and upset about all of these details. There's only one thing you need. And Mary has made the right choice. She has chosen the one thing, and it will not be taken away from her."

Mary had breached a barrier by sitting in the men's space. And on top of that, she sat in the posture of a disciple. Every teacher before or since had only male disciples. Jesus was the uncommon exception. He welcomed women to be His disciples also.

I was impressed that the Teacher defended Mary. I was equally impressed with His tenderness toward Martha, disarming her by saying her name twice.

Martha's face relaxed. She dropped her chin slightly, unfolded her arms, and walked slowly back into the courtyard.

I could tell Martha was embarrassed. The Teacher's words left a wound for several days. It was especially difficult for Martha to accept the added praise that Jesus gave to Mary. But she eventually came to terms with what He said, and she was never the same. Afterward, she was less distracted, less worried, less agitated.

～◈～

When Jesus finished His teaching, Martha signaled that the meal was ready. He then did something equally surprising. He asked us to all eat together—women and men—in the public room.

Mary and Martha hesitated. They looked at one another with raised eyebrows. Jesus' followers weren't fazed; they had seen Him break customs before. So all of us—Mary and Martha included—ate together.

My sisters had prepared a marvelous meal that day. Platters containing piles of flatbread, fish, goat cheese, olives, eggs, and dried figs, along with pitchers of goat milk, wine, and bowls of lentil stew filled the table.

I will never forget the Teacher's words to Martha:

"One thing is needful … and I won't take it away from Mary."

These words stirred in my mind all evening.

Later that night, I asked Jesus to elaborate on them. And I recall Him saying the following in response:

"Hearing My word is more important than service. Following is more important than working. Martha tended to My physical needs, but Mary tended to that which is most important to Me: being My apprentice.

"Mary received Me into her heart long before she received Me into Your home," Jesus continued. "She laid all other things aside and gave heed to My words. And she made this her only task.

"Martha has the heart of a servant, but all service for Me must flow from communion with Me. Martha absorbed herself with the bread that perishes; Mary was nourishing herself with the bread from heaven, which shall never perish.

"To obey is better than sacrifice. The primary task of a disciple is to learn of Me. Worry not, Lazarus. Martha will learn this also."

At that moment, it dawned on me that Jesus wasn't just a teacher—He was a prophet: one who carried God's Word.

Martha's hospitality was important. But it was focused on the temporal. Mary's hospitality was more important because the greatest way to welcome a prophet is to receive His words. And this was what Mary did.

In the days that followed, we all came to understand that Jesus was much more than a teacher and a prophet. He was the Messiah of God.

The Teacher and His disciples lodged with us that night. He talked with me for hours when the others retired to sleep. I am a reserved, unobtrusive person. I do not say much. But being with the Teacher made me feel at ease. I could ask Him whatever was on my mind without fear.

For reasons that I do not grasp, Jesus took a liking to me. I was honored and amazed at the same time. I never had a brother of my own, but He felt close to one.

I would later learn that Jesus was in fact my elder brother … and a friend who sticks closer than any natural sibling. As it says in Proverbs,

> A man of many companions may come to ruin, but there is a friend who sticks closer than a brother.[2]

So that is what took place the first time Jesus stepped into our home. There would be many other occasions where we were graced with the calm majesty of His presence and heard the mighty and mysterious words that fell from His lips.

As often as He would climb the dust-paved road from Jericho and depart from the golden gates of the holy city of Jerusalem, He would visit us in Bethany.

In fact, Jesus would never spend a night in the holy city; He would lodge only with us.

Our house was always open to Him and His followers.

He was not just our Teacher, our Lord, and our Savior. He was an intimate and beloved friend—*our* friend.

It always seemed to delight His heart to gladden our home with His presence.

We were filled with an unutterable love for Him. And we knew that He loved us even more.

This became clear to all of us after I became ill …

THE SACRED TEXT

Now it happened as they went that He entered a certain village; and a certain woman named Martha welcomed Him into her house. And she had a sister called Mary, who also sat at Jesus' feet and heard His word. But Martha was distracted with much serving, and she approached Him and said, "Lord, do You not care that my sister has left me to serve alone? Therefore tell her to help me." And Jesus answered and said to her, "Martha, Martha, you are worried and troubled about many things. But one thing is needed, and Mary has chosen that good part, which will not be taken away from her."

—Luke 10:38–42 NKJV

WALKING IT OUT

Hast thou heard Him, seen Him, known Him?
Is not thine a captured heart?
Chief among ten thousand own Him;
Joyful choose the better part.

Consider the striking contrast between the village of Bethany and the holy city of Jerusalem during the time of Jesus.

It's like comparing the corner grocery store to the Super Mall.

The population of Bethany couldn't have been more than four hundred people. A scant two miles away, Jerusalem had a population of fifty to sixty thousand. During the religious festivals, the population of the holy city could reach up to the hundreds of thousands.

Compare the two locations in your mind.

Jerusalem—the holy city of David contained intoxicating crowds, formed the center of Israel's worship, and featured a fully robed priesthood. The city was fast-paced, throbbing, exciting, restless, and hectic. Jerusalem also boasted the presence of the great temple, clothed in stunning gold.

Within walking distance, almost in the shadow of the temple walls, was the lowly town of Bethany—obscure, unknown, modest.

In which of these two places did the God of the universe feel at home?

The tiny village of Bethany.

This example screams that God is more concerned with quality than with quantity. It shouts that He's more concerned with reality than with flash. It thunders that He's more concerned with authentic hearts than with what's outwardly impressive.

Jesus of Nazareth, the Son of God, was bitterly rejected by the world. But He was gladly received in Bethany.

> Now it came to pass, as they went, that he entered into a certain village: and a certain woman named Martha received him into her house.[3]

Thank God for Martha. She received the Lord Jesus into her home. She welcomed Him into her family.

This leads to a significant question. What does it mean to properly receive the Lord Jesus in our day?

How to Properly Receive Christ

Every Christian on the planet claims that they receive Jesus. But what does it mean to *properly* receive Him?

It seems to me that there are three key aspects involved in the proper reception of the Lord Jesus, all of which are often overlooked today.

(1) To receive Christ is to receive all that He is

Some Christians receive Jesus as the Justifier but reject Him as the *Justice-giver*. By contrast, some emphasize His role of bringing justice to the world but downplay His role of justifying sinners.

But Jesus Christ is both Justifier and Justice-giver.

Some want Christ's ministry of building up and deepening Christian community but reject His ministry of reaching the lost. Others reverse the order. To their minds, evangelism is essential while community is optional.

To receive Christ in this partial fashion is to receive Him on our own terms. It is to create a Jesus after our own image rather than welcoming Him for who He really is.

To properly receive Jesus Christ is to receive *all* that He is. He is a whole Person. We cannot take one part of Him and reject the other parts. As E. Stanley Jones once said, "A reduced Christ is the same as a rejected Christ."

Bethany is the place where Jesus Christ—*the whole Christ*—was and is welcomed and received.

(2) To receive Christ is to receive all who are a part of Him

Jesus said to His disciples, "He who receives you receives me."[4] Paul said, "Therefore receive one another, just as Christ also received us, to the glory of God."[5]

To receive a person whom Christ has received is to receive Christ Himself. And to reject someone whom Christ has received is to reject Christ Himself.

This means that any Christian or church that welcomes some members of the Body, but rejects others, is rejecting Christ Himself.

Paul said as much in his first letter to the Corinthians:

> The eye cannot say to the hand, "I don't need you!" And the head cannot say to the feet, "I don't need you!" On the contrary, those parts of the body that seem to be weaker are indispensable, and the parts that we think are less honorable we treat with special honor. And the parts that are unpresentable are treated with special modesty.[6]

In Bethany, all who have received Christ are received into fellowship. They are all welcomed.

To do otherwise is to say, "Lord, we'll take Your hand and Your arm, but we don't want Your foot or Your leg."

To be exclusive in this way is to dismember Jesus Christ.[7] This makes the healing of leprosy even more symbolically powerful when you consider the rotting away of limbs.

Don't misunderstand. I'm not saying that we should welcome people's sins or empower them in doing evil. I'm talking about welcoming people while rejecting their sin. I'm talking about receiving all of those who are in Christ, all of those whom Christ has received.

The fact is: Jesus receives all who are His. And He welcomes all who are seeking Him.

Recall that when our Lord was on earth, He laid out the welcome mat to all kinds of shabby characters who were shunned by the pious, including prostitutes, tax collectors, lepers, Gentiles, and Samaritans. In His day, eating signified communion, solidarity, and fellowship. Jesus welcomed sinners at His table as well as self-righteous Pharisees.

Exclusivism and narrowness betray the spirit of Bethany, and they expose the fact that the Lord has not been fully received.

In short, the Lord is looking for a people by whom He is completely received and fully welcomed. Not Christ plus something else, and not Christ minus a part of Himself. *He is looking for a people who welcome Christ as all and in all.*[8]

As I've said and written elsewhere, sectarianism and elitism are like body odor. Everyone else can smell it except those who have it.

Sectarianism and elitism are religiously transmitted diseases that appear symptomless to those who have them. So be sure to take into consideration the testimony of others on this point.

Make no mistake about it: Jesus Christ does not feel at home in a Christian or in a church that is sectarian or elitist.

And the root of both is self-righteousness, which trumps every other kind of sin.

(3) To receive Christ is to give Him first place

> For by Him all things were created, both in the heavens and on earth, visible and invisible, whether thrones or dominions or rulers or authorities—all things have been created through Him and for Him ... so that He Himself will come to have first place in everything.[9]

Ever since I became a Christian, I've met countless believers who treated their lives like the US government treats its various departments.

In the US government, there is the Department of Education, the Department of Homeland Security, the Department of Agriculture, the Department of Defense, etc.

In the same way, I know many Christians who compartmentalize their lives into the department of family, the department of career, the department of hobbies, the department of entertainment, the department of religion, etc.

For them, Jesus is the head of the department of religion. And that department is separated from the other departments of their lives.

The "religious" part of their lives is what they do on Sunday morning. But the rest of their lives, including most of the books they read (for example), has nothing to do with Jesus. They get their excitement and zest for life elsewhere. For many, the goal of living is to make money, send their kids to college, and enjoy their children or grandchildren.

The New Testament, however, gives us a completely different picture. Jesus is Lord of all and Lord over all. That includes the totality of our lives. And for the devoted follower of Christ, Jesus and the things that relate to Him become their zest for living.

Making loads of money, sending one's children to college, and having grandchildren—as good as those things may be— are not the hallmarks of the kingdom of God.

There is much more to life than living, bearing offspring, and dying. As Christians, we have a glorious destiny to fulfill that goes beyond ourselves.

God the Father has given Jesus the highest place—*total supremacy*—in all things. So the lordship of Jesus must touch every part of our lives, including what we read, listen to, talk about, and watch. His lordship must also inform the values that govern our day-to-day decisions.

In Ephesians, Paul wrote the following prayer:

> … that He would grant you, according to the riches of
> His glory, to be strengthened with power through His

Spirit in the inner man, so that Christ may dwell in your
hearts through faith ...[10]

The Greek word translated "dwell" in this text does not
simply mean to live in or take up residency. Rather, it means to
make one's home in and to settle down.

Jesus indwells all believers by His Spirit. But He seeks to
make His home and settle down in our hearts. That is, He
wants a Bethany. And that requires that we give Him the highest place in our lives.

Choosing the Better Part

Some Bible commentators have engaged in Martha-bashing.
Others have engaged in Mary-bashing.

Mary is often depicted as being "too heavenly minded to be
any earthly good." She selfishly listened to Jesus teach, leaving
her sister behind to do the heavy lifting. Mary is said to be
the woman who worships God in her living room with hands
raised while she ignores the knock on the door from the hungry neighbor who is without food.

Martha is often depicted as a domestic diva—the first-
century equivalent to Martha Stewart—her idol being
domestic performance. Martha wanted to impress Jesus with
a great meal but cared little about hearing Him teach. She is

said to be the woman who is too earthly-minded to be any heavenly good.

Both of these Sunday school portraits are dead wrong, and they should be put to the torch.

The truth is that Mary helped Martha with the meal preparations. She didn't avoid the "kitchen duties."

Martha's initial complaint verifies that observation. Martha said that Mary "left me."[11] You can't leave someone unless they were already with you.

Mary received Jesus on a higher plane than did her dutiful sister. Jesus was not after mere domestic performance. Listening to His teaching honored Him more than attending to His physical needs.

The Greek text tells us that Mary "kept on listening to His word." Jesus wanted to pour that which was in His own heart into the hearts of those listening. He was looking for people who would eagerly receive and understand what He had to say.

Mary was such an open vessel. Only by being a listening disciple can one be a proper hostess. But there is something more.

In Jesus' day, homes were divided into the male space and the female space. The kitchen (typically the courtyard) was the domain of the women. The public room was the domain of the men.

For a woman to settle down in the public room with the men was culturally awkward and offensive.

The only two places that were shared by both the men and the women were the marital bedroom and outside the house where the children played.

Mary crossed an invisible line. By entering the public room, she breached two social boundaries. First, she sat in the men's space. Second, she sat in the posture of a disciple.

A disciple in the first century wasn't someone who learned academically, as if to listen to a lecture, take notes, and study them. A disciple was an apprentice—a person who was learning a way of life. The first lesson of Christian discipleship is to sit under the Lord Jesus and learn from Him.

So when Mary sat at Jesus' feet in the public room, it constituted no small scandal. She took the posture of a disciple.[12] Every rabbi in that day had only male disciples. Jesus was the uncommon exception. He welcomed women to be His disciples also. Including women as full-fledged disciples was a testament to the radical nature of His ministry.

As far as we know, Jesus was also the first Jewish teacher to have women (unrelated by blood) as part of His traveling entourage of disciples.[13] And for a Jewish woman to leave her home and travel with a teacher was scandalous.

In her bitter accusation, Martha was in effect saying, "My sister is in the public room, acting like a man, when she should be in the courtyard helping me!"

While we can understand Martha's complaint against her sister on a human level, it was undeserved and unkind.

I'm impressed that not a single word of defense fell from Mary's lips. Instead, Jesus rose to her defense, affirming her right to learn from Him.

Martha, seeking to serve the Lord according to her own thoughts, was distracted and diverted. The Greek word translated "distracted" in Luke 10:40 means to be preoccupied, pulled in different directions, or driven about mentally.

Anytime we seek to serve the Lord according to our own ideas and in our own energy, we—*like Martha*—are bound to exhibit a failed temper and frayed nerves.

An agitated and aggravated Martha ascribed blame to Jesus, reproving Him for not caring.

Jesus' rebuke to Martha was kind. This is revealed in the fact that He repeated her name twice. Naming someone twice indicated concern, tenderness, and seriousness. The other examples in the Bible make this clear: "Simon, Simon";[14]

"Saul, Saul";[15] "Oh Jerusalem, Jerusalem";[16] "My God, my God."[17]

Note that Jesus never denigrated or belittled the value of Martha's work. Jesus loved Martha, and we should commend her for receiving Him into her home. A single fault shouldn't erase her noble character.

The Lord simply put His finger on a subtle problem. Martha's service required reorientation. Fretting and fussing, Martha was troubled by "many things," occupied with her "much serving." Jesus was saying, in effect, "You are putting yourself into a needless uproar."

> "Martha, Martha, you are worried and troubled about
> many things. But one thing is needed …"[18]

Martha's service, though well-motivated, was misguided and misdirected. So Jesus contrasted the "many things" with the "one thing" that was needed. The "one thing" is Christ Himself. And the better thing is to be His disciple.

In *Jesus Manifesto*, I expound on this thought, issuing a clarion call for all Christians to center on Jesus Christ rather than the countless religious rabbit trails that distract us from Him. Even trails of ministry and service can easily become distractions.

I'm not suggesting complacency or insensitivity to the needs of the world. God forbid. The issue is that our chief priority is to get to know Jesus Christ and learn to live by Him.

To put it another way, our service to the Lord should originate from the Lord's clear direction. He will put people on our hearts, sometimes burdening us to pray for, speak to, or serve them in some way. When that happens, we should act—*not trusting in ourselves*—but relying wholly on His power and ability.

Thus it is possible to be outwardly busy serving God *while* we sit at the feet of Jesus. The caution here is against serving the Lord anxiously with all that we have yet failing to be His disciple. Being a disciple is about following the Lord's leading and doing what He tells us to do.

"One thing is needful," the Lord said. "And I won't take it away from her."

Mary's attention was riveted on "one thing." And both the psalmist and Paul spoke about it:

> One thing I ask of the LORD, this is what I seek: that I may dwell in the house of the LORD all the days of my life, to gaze upon the beauty of the LORD and to seek him in his temple.[19]

> Brothers, I do not consider myself yet to have taken hold of it. But one thing I do: Forgetting what is behind and straining toward what is ahead, I press on toward the

> goal to win the prize for which God has called me heavenward in Christ Jesus.[20]

Paul lost "all things" to gain the "one thing."

> What is more, I consider everything a loss compared to the surpassing greatness of knowing Christ Jesus my Lord, for whose sake I have lost all things. I consider them rubbish, that I may gain Christ.[21]

Shattering a False Dichotomy

Beginning from the mid-third century onward, Christian writers have used Martha and Mary as models for the two main personalities in the church: the busy activists (the Marthas) and the quiet reflectives (the Marys).

As an observer of the passing parade, I don't believe this caricature fits the biblical story. While I think it might describe Martha fairly well, it misses the mark when it comes to Mary.

Let me explain.

There is no question that Martha saw her service to Jesus as an act of love and worship. The fact that Jesus never belittled her service toward Him confirms this.

However, some Martha-types have a way of reducing a relationship with God to feverish activity. Such people obsess over how many lost people you've shared Christ with, what you're doing to help the poor and oppressed, how involved you are in social justice and making the world a better place. In their minds, all of these things are the badges of being a "good Christian."

But to my everlasting astonishment, most of the Marys I've met in my life used to be Marthas. They just burned out or bailed out.

Let's talk about those who burned out. These former Marthas didn't know how to say no when asked to participate in various church programs, activities, and ministries. They were constantly busy, serving every spare moment they had. In their eyes, serving at the church or staying busy with ministry activities was the equivalent of loving God.

Guilt, condemnation, religious duty, and obligation subtly motivated and governed their activities. They were trying to win brownie points with a God who stopped keeping score two thousand years ago.

There came a point, however, when the weight of Christian service simply crushed them. And burnout ensued.

Some Marthas went beyond burnout and bailed out. They felt they had served God with all they had. But when they observed others who were blessed by God, yet who weren't as "faithful," they grew bitter and abandoned the Lord.

"I'm doing all this for You, yet You're blessing them instead," was their bitter cry.

Some of these people later repented and returned to the Lord, acknowledging that their service to God was more about them instead of Him.

In both cases, these Marthas realized that they had confused service with a relationship with Jesus. They made the profound yet painful discovery that they had been serving the idol of "service" rather than God Himself.

They also discovered that the source of their service—the strength they relied upon to serve God—was not the life of Christ. The source was their own natural strength and energy.

What is more, they realized that their very identities and security were wrapped up in their service. That's why they craved attention for their work. It's also why they became a critic and a judge of the service (or non-service) of others.

The result: after slaving as Marthas for many years, they became Marys. That is, they learned to rest in Christ, hear His voice, and draw on His energy for ministry.

Again, Mary was not someone who lacked in service. Jesus had no word of rebuke or complaint for her. And as we've already seen, Mary helped Martha before Jesus moved into teaching mode.

The antidote, therefore, is not for Marys to move closer to being Marthas (to serve more). Nor is it for Marthas to move closer to being Marys (to worship more). This isn't a question of balance. It's a question of priority, orientation, and source.

All service must flow from communion with the Lord if it is to have lasting value. All service must find its source in the life of Christ so it won't lead to burnout or bail-out.

> Unless the LORD builds the house, its builders labor in vain.[22]

All service must flow out of a razor-sharp desire to please God rather than a desire to get noticed by others. If it does not, it will lead to either complaint or criticism.

When God created the world, He worked for six days and then rested. Adam was created on the sixth day. So God's seventh day—*the Sabbath*—was Adam's first full day.

God works before He rests. Humans, however, rest before they work. This principle undergirds all Christian service. We rest in Christ before we work for Christ. Or in the language of Ephesians, we sit before we stand or walk.[23]

> For anyone who enters God's rest also rests from his own work, just as God did from his.[24]

Mary is our example in all of these things. And she has the defense of Jesus to confirm it.

In short, it's a dangerous thing to be so busy for the Lord that you don't have time to seek Him and wait on His direction.

Acting "religious" is the fallen soul's way of trying to duplicate the job of the Holy Spirit.

∽◎∼

There is room for all human temperaments in the body of Christ. The Lord uses the choleric, practical, outspoken, and assertive activists as well as the phlegmatic, calm, contemplative, timid, and docile pacifists.

But while God doesn't do away with our unique temperaments and personalities, He wishes to adjust them so that they are in line with His character, directed by His will, and energized by His life.

An Audience of One

There's a great deal of ego bound up with Christian ministry today. And all who labor for the Lord can fall prey to it. But impressing people isn't the name of the game. Today's heroes are tomorrow's zeroes. The story of Paul and Barnabas in Lystra teaches us this lesson in spades.

The story is found in Acts 14:11–19. In the space of nine verses, the same people who set out to worship Paul and Barnabas were ready to send them to their deaths.

What changed their minds about the two apostles so rapidly? The "evil report" (rumors) leveled by Paul's detractors in Pisidian Antioch and Iconium.

Such is the nature of fallen mortals.

With that in view, here are some things that will help us keep perspective about who we're actually serving:

Make a decision to live unto God rather than unto humans. Seek to please Him alone. As difficult as it is, lay down the desire to be a "human pleaser." If you live to please humans, you'll have your reward here and now.[25] Learn the lesson of Lystra. Some who will sing your praises today will end up condemning you tomorrow. There are only five minutes between the compliment and the insult. As Kipling once put it in his poem *If*, triumph and disaster are two impostors that should be treated the same.

Ambition to become something great in the eyes of your fellow Christians and ambition to please the Lord are two very different things. True servanthood demands neither help nor attention. Deny the carnal temptation to impress mortals. Don't worry about doing great feats for God. Instead, focus on taking steps to respond to Him in obedience. Those steps will add up eventually.

If you see someone doing or saying something that inspires and encourages you in the Lord, let them know about it. You don't know what difference it could make in their lives.

It may be a needed word given at the right moment. One of my spiritual disciplines (practices) is to express gratitude and appreciation to those who have touched or enriched my life in some way. I try to never let that slip.

An exhortation from one beggar to another: keep sacrificing. Keep losing. Keep laying your life down. Keep loving your enemies. Keep blessing those who despise you. Keep refusing to return fire upon those who bad-mouth you. Keep pouring your life into others, even if those people never acknowledge it and even if others never notice. Keep faithfully serving your Lord without looking back. Why? Because there is One who is watching. And only His opinion matters.

B. J. Hoff put it beautifully: "It matters not if the world has heard or approves or understands … the only applause we're meant to seek is that of nail-scarred hands."

Notice how Jesus connected having faith with seeking God's approval alone:

> How can you believe if you accept praise from one another, yet make no effort to obtain the praise that comes from the only God?[26]

To lose sight of this is to live on the human level where numbers, praises, and applause determine your happiness.

Learn to live before an Audience of One. May this be the hallmark of your life.

Mary knew this lesson well. And Martha eventually discovered it.

∽⦿⤸

So from this brief narrative, we discover several features about Bethany.

In Bethany Jesus Christ is completely received.

In Bethany, our chief priority is to sit at the Lord's feet, hear His word, and respond.

In Bethany, our service flows from our communion with Christ. This is the source from which we receive His direction and draw upon His strength.

In Bethany, women are given the same privileges and the same status to be disciples as men.

In Bethany, our temperaments, dispositions, and motives are exposed, and transformation occurs.

In Bethany, we live for an Audience of One.

The Lord's call for all of us in this hour is simply … *be a Bethany.*

Yet there are more lessons bound up in this little village …

Chapter 3

AWAKENED IN BETHANY

Time crept by. There was still no sign of Jesus. I had fallen ill. The eastern fever raged through me, roasting my body from the inside out.

It had been two weeks since the onset of the disease. And my condition worsened by the day.

When I could no longer walk, my sisters sent word to Jesus through a messenger. They knew the Teacher was staying on the east side of the Jordan River in the region of Perea, and they sent the following word to Him:

"Teacher, the one whom You love is seriously ill."

That same evening my fever worsened. My limbs refused to obey my feeble commands. I could scarcely sit up. The bed became a prison for my failing body.

My sisters were overwhelmed with the bitter prospect that I would not recover. Martha complained, "If the Teacher were here, Lazarus would be healed."

I heard Mary mutter, "Jesus has to come."

My father continued to encourage me. Jesus had healed him; surely He would heal me also.

I could not sleep most of the night. Tossing miserably, my mind refused to shut down. Neither would the pain vibrating throughout my body.

If I die, what will happen to my sisters ... and my father? With the silversmith shop closed, who will provide for them? These were the worries that tormented my mind.

That evening my three closest friends, Nathan, Samuel, and Tobias, paid me a visit.

I opened my eyes at the pounding of feet up the stairs toward my room.

After the men entered, they each stood around my bed and began to speak.

Nathan leaned forward, his face the picture of sadness. Somberly he said, "Lazarus, you know that I lost my faith in God years ago. Like you, I was taught from childhood that

YHWH would deliver our people from our oppressors. But there have been no signs of it. Not just for my generation, but for generations before me.

"All I see around me is pain, oppression, evil. And now here you are, a righteous man who loves God, sick and ready to die. Your sickness only confirms my doubts. A man must die with integrity. I want to encourage you, then, to give up your faith and die with integrity."

Nathan stopped, and we looked at one another for a brief moment. I didn't answer him.

Shaking his head in disagreement, Samuel leaned close to me and said, "Lazarus, as you know, I do not agree with our friend Nathan. I believe YHWH's promises are true and the Messiah is coming to deliver us. But you are mistaken to believe that Jesus of Nazareth is the Messiah.

"If Jesus truly was the person He claims to be, where is He when you need Him most? If He was truly a prophet, He would have known about your sickness and healed you. I don't want you to die in a state of deception. Renounce your faith in Jesus and repent to God for believing this imposter. I believe God will forgive you if you do. There is still time."

Tobias drew back, his face blank. "You know I love you, Lazarus," he whispered.

I nodded.

"And what I'm about to say is with the kindest of intentions. We know that God heals the righteous and afflicts the sinful. This sickness has come upon you for a reason. There is something in your life, some unconfessed or unrepented sin with which you have not yet dealt.

"I want you to get well. I beg you, therefore, to search your heart. Confess the sin that you have committed and seek redemption. I am assured that if you do this, God will heal you."

I was speechless. The pain in my body moved to my heart. My friends meant well, but their words brought little comfort.

My muscles froze. I willed my face to turn to stone. I didn't want my emotions to show. My lips tightened. Devastated, the heart-wrenching was almost too much for me.

It took me a little time to regain my composure. Still lying flat on my back, I mustered up the strength to open my mouth. Their accusations still raged through my mind as I groped for an appropriate response.

"Friends, I know you all mean well. But I will tell you what is on my heart right now."

I turned to Nathan. "I know that the God of our fathers lives, Nathan. Even though I cannot see it now, I believe He will fulfill His promises one day just as He always has. His timetable is not like ours. I will die trusting in the God of Abraham, Isaac, and Jacob."

Nathan's face sank into his chest.

At this point my throat tightened. Struggling to breathe, I looked into Samuel's eyes and said, "I admit that I do not understand why Jesus hasn't come to me yet. And I know that if He were here, I would be healed.

"But I trust Him, nonetheless. And I believe with all my heart that He is the promised One, the Messiah, the Son of the living God. Of that I am sure. I expect Him to come and heal me soon. But even if He does not, I will die believing that He is the One to come."

My heart pounded harder.

I looked over at Tobias. "Tobias, I have searched my heart before God, and I do not believe that there is anything I have done to bring this illness upon me. I cannot explain to you why I am sick. If I die, I will do so believing that I have not sinned against my God."

My arms and hands went numb. My legs quickly followed.

With my hand I motioned to Nathan to move his head near mine. "Call my sisters and father," I whispered in his ear.

Mary, Martha, and my father rushed up the steps to my room. I looked at each of them with love in my eyes, struggling to utter my parting words. Martha's hands trembled. Tears slid down her cheeks. Mary sobbed on the shoulder of my father.

I could feel the blood leave my face. But before I could say a word, I fell asleep.

I died in their presence.

The rest of the story was recalled to me by my sisters, my father, and John, the Teacher's disciple.

Mary and Martha were crestfallen.

The messenger arrived that evening. My sisters wept heavily in my room. My father ordered that my body be taken to the grave.

The messenger told Mary and Martha that Jesus' only response to their message was: "The ultimate end of this sickness is not death. It is for God's glory so that the Son of God may be glorified."

Feeling that this was callous disregard on the Teacher's part, Martha's weeping grew louder, and she said to Mary, "I feel lied to. Jesus said that Lazarus would not die. Why … why did this happen!? How could He let it happen!?"

Mary, weeping in bewilderment, hugged Martha and said, "I'm perplexed too, but don't let bitterness grip your heart. There must be an explanation. The Teacher will come and tell us why. I know He will."

Martha's disappointment moved to bossiness: "If He doesn't show up for the burial tonight, I am not sure if I can forgive Him. That will be too much for me to bear."

Martha oversaw the funeral arrangements that evening. She covered my body in myrrh and aloes to fight off the stench of death. Strips of fine linen wrapped my body. They placed me in a sealed tomb, closed off from the world of the living.

Our friends and family from Jerusalem gave their loving support. Mourners were hired. Mary and Martha were grieved beyond measure.

Three days passed. Our home was filled with friends and family, all weeping, grieving, and mourning their loss.

Martha was in the courtyard when one of our friends ran to her with a message. Out of breath, our friend said, "Jesus is on His way to Bethany! His disciples are with Him, and they are just outside the village!"

Martha's pan clattered to the floor. She ran out of the courtyard to greet Jesus at the outskirts of Bethany.

Martha slid to a stop. With tears running down her cheeks, she cried violently, "Lord, if You had been here, my brother would not have died! Yet even now that he is dead, I know that God will grant You whatever You ask."

Jesus responded, "Your brother will rise again from the dead."

Martha shook her head and recoiled. "I know he will rise on the last day when the dead are resurrected."

Not breaking His gaze from hers, Jesus replied, "You believe the dead will rise again. That is right. But I am the Resurrection and the Life. The person who believes in Me, though he or she dies, shall live. And whoever lives and believes in Me shall never taste death. Do you believe this?"

Martha stood silent. She raised her head and said, "I believe You are the Messiah, the Son of God, the promised One to come."

Martha's shoulders slumped. Her sorrow-stricken spirit was not able to digest the fact that Jesus claimed to hold the keys of death in His hands. Not just for the future, but for the present.

Jesus asked, "Where is Mary? I would like to speak with her." Martha replied, "I will get her for You."

Martha quickly ran back to the house, where Mary sat on the floor, weeping under the weight of her grief.

Hoping not to be heard by the others, Martha whispered into Mary's ear, "The Teacher is outside the village, and He is asking for you."

Surprised, Mary straightened and ran out to meet Him. Friends and neighbors trailed after her. They assumed she was running to visit my tomb.

When Mary saw Jesus, she wilted to her knees and dissolved into tears. Broken with hopeless grief, she echoed Martha's words: "If You had been here, my brother would not have died."

Jesus took her hand and lifted her to her feet. Deeply stirred by the sight of Mary's sorrow, He sighed. With deep shuddering emotion, Jesus asked her, "Where have you laid his body?"

The Teacher visibly shook. Then He burst into tears.

The sight of Mary's tears brought tears to the face of God's Son.

No words could give comfort to Mary. Only the gesture of a weeping Messiah would suffice.

Groaning inwardly and weeping outwardly, Jesus made His way to the tomb. Mary and the Teacher's disciples accompanied Him. Those who followed Mary to where Jesus was walked behind.

Upon seeing His tears, one of the Jews who followed murmured, "See how He loved Lazarus. He opened the eyes of the blind. So couldn't He have kept Lazarus from dying?"

They entered the village, and Mary fetched both Martha and my father. They all approached the tomb together.

With majestic composure, Jesus commanded that the stone be removed from the tomb.

Martha, who had prepared me for burial, gasped in surprise. "Lord, he has been dead four days. By this time his body will stink," she anxiously protested.

Trusting the Teacher, Mary was silent.

Jesus mildly yet firmly reproved Martha, reminding her of something He had said previously. "Did I not tell you that you would see God's glory if you only believed?"

Martha, not understanding, hung her head and fell silent.

Nathan, Samuel, and several other men put their hands on the large stone that covered the mouth of the tomb. They pushed upon it until it was unseated from the groove in the ground that held it in place. The mouth of the tomb stood open and exposed.

Everyone watched with anticipation. Some pinched their noses, thinking that Jesus would ask that my body be brought out into the open.

Jesus tilted His head back, raised His eyes to the heavens, and prayed.

Speaking to His Father in heaven, He said that He did not need to pray out loud. But for the sake of those around Him, He wanted everyone to know that the Father had sent Him.

With those words, He lowered His head and fixed His gaze on the tomb where I lay. Jesus was now ready to bare His arm of insuperable power and unsurpassed grandeur to a crowd hushed with breathless expectation.

I heard the voice of the Teacher shouting to me … that voice that I knew so well. His piercing cry jolted me back to consciousness. I felt as though I were in a deep sleep, but the sound of His voice … a voice that I instantly recognized … woke me out of it.

"Lazarus, come forth!"

I suddenly gasped for breath.

When I realized I was conscious, I tried to open my eyes. But it was too difficult because the headcloth was wound so tightly around my face.

I had feeling in my entire body, but I was still bandaged from head to toe. The bandages around my legs were loose enough for me to manipulate them slightly. So I managed to wiggle and worm until I could get on my feet. Lurching toward the light, the noise of the crowd helped me find my way toward the entrance.

As soon as I was in view of the crowd, I could hear the shrieks and screams of those who saw me.

"It's a ghost!" some gasped.

"That's not … that's not Lazarus … it's impossible!" another yelled.

Gripped by awe, they were mortified.

A dead man had been raised to life right before their eyes.

It was a scene of peerless wonder and unrivaled glory.

I heard the voice of Jesus again. This time He commanded that I be unwrapped and set free.

Nathan and Samuel rushed over to me and began unwrapping my bandages. Nathan shouted, "There's no stench! Jesus caused the corruption to move into reverse."

The insufferable heat warmed my cold body. Beads of sweat began to form on my arms and forehead.

Once they removed the headcloth, I tried to open my eyes. But I could only squint as the blinding sun seared my eyes. My body ached, but the illness was gone. The pain had vanished.

Mary, Martha, and my father embraced one another, weeping. Joyful amazement was written upon their faces. I turned my hands over, unable to comprehend the gift I had just been given.

Martha ran over to me, grasped my arms, and stared wide-eyed at me. "Lazarus!" she said. I replied, "Yes, sister, it is me. I am alive!"

Martha looked a little different. The sorrow had transfigured her face.

Jesus remained unruffled and composed. I walked over to Him, and we embraced one another. "Lord," I said, "thank You. I believe You are the Son of God, the Promised Messiah."

Still arrested by the spectacle, many of the people surged forward, reaching out their hands to touch me. Some of them ran to Jerusalem to report what they had witnessed.

We retreated back to our home in Bethany. Jesus and His disciples remained with us for a few days. A steady stream of people came to visit us. They wanted to see me with their own eyes, proving to themselves that I was in fact alive.

"Lazarus, we have to leave today."

The early sun peeked through the olive tree, caressing the Teacher's face as he announced the news. "There is a plot afoot to kill Me. The Judeans want me dead. So I can no longer move freely. We will travel to the countryside near Ephraim. But I will return."

I nodded my head. Disappointed that He was leaving, I said, "I will look forward to Your return. We all will."

The following weeks were unforgettable. People visited Bethany just to gaze at me. Some would ask me for favors so they could observe me carefully, perhaps to make sure that I was real and not a spirit.

As I reflected on the events of that day, I not only witnessed the power of Jesus' resurrection life. But also His brilliance. He asked for others to remove the stone in order to prove that what He was about to do was neither a fraud nor a fake.

I am thankful that He brought me back to life. Not only so that I could witness His own resurrected body. But so that I could also witness something that happened just before He died. The immortal act that my sister Mary would perform ...

THE SACRED TEXT

Now a man named Lazarus was sick. He was from Bethany, the village of Mary and her sister Martha. (This Mary, whose brother Lazarus now lay sick, was the same one who poured perfume on the Lord and wiped his feet with her hair.) So the sisters sent word to Jesus, "Lord, the one you love is sick."

When he heard this, Jesus said, "This sickness will not end in death. No, it is for God's glory so that God's Son may be glorified through it." Now Jesus loved Martha and her sister and Lazarus. So when he heard that Lazarus was sick, he stayed where he was two more days, and then he said to his disciples, "Let us go back to Judea."

"But Rabbi," they said, "a short while ago the Jews there tried to stone you, and yet you are going back?"

Jesus answered, "Are there not twelve hours of daylight? Anyone who walks in the daytime will not stumble, for they see by this world's light. It is when a person walks at night that they stumble, for they have no light."

After he had said this, he went on to tell them, "Our friend Lazarus has fallen asleep; but I am going there to wake him up."

His disciples replied, "Lord, if he sleeps, he will get better." Jesus had been speaking of his death, but his disciples thought he meant natural sleep.

So then he told them plainly, "Lazarus is dead, and for your sake I am glad I was not there, so that you may believe. But let us go to him."

Then Thomas (also known as Didymus) said to the rest of the disciples, "Let us also go, that we may die with him."

On his arrival, Jesus found that Lazarus had already been in the tomb for four days. Now Bethany was less than two miles from Jerusalem, and many Jews had come to Martha and Mary to comfort them in the loss of their brother. When Martha heard that Jesus was coming, she went out to meet him, but Mary stayed at home.

"Lord," Martha said to Jesus, "if you had been here, my brother would not have died. But I know that even now God will give you whatever you ask."

Jesus said to her, "Your brother will rise again."

Martha answered, "I know he will rise again in the resurrection at the last day."

Jesus said to her, "I am the resurrection and the life. The one who believes in me will live, even though they die; and whoever lives by believing in me will never die. Do you believe this?"

"Yes, Lord," she replied, "I believe that you are the Messiah, the Son of God, who is to come into the world."

After she had said this, she went back and called her sister Mary aside. "The Teacher is here," she said, "and is asking for you." When Mary heard this, she got up quickly and went to him. Now Jesus had not yet entered the village, but was still at the place where Martha had met him. When the Jews who had been with Mary in the house, comforting her, noticed how quickly she got up and went out, they followed her, supposing she was going to the tomb to mourn there.

When Mary reached the place where Jesus was and saw him, she fell at his feet and said, "Lord, if you had been here, my brother would not have died."

When Jesus saw her weeping, and the Jews who had come along with her also weeping, he was deeply moved in spirit and troubled. "Where have you laid him?" he asked.

"Come and see, Lord," they replied.

Jesus wept.

Then the Jews said, "See how he loved him!"

But some of them said, "Could not he who opened the eyes of the blind man have kept this man from dying?"

Jesus, once more deeply moved, came to the tomb. It was a cave with a stone laid across the entrance. "Take away the stone," he said.

"But, Lord," said Martha, the sister of the dead man, "by this time there is a bad odor, for he has been there four days."

Then Jesus said, "Did I not tell you that if you believe, you will see the glory of God?"

So they took away the stone. Then Jesus looked up and said, "Father, I thank you that you have heard me. I knew that you always hear me, but I said this for the benefit of the people standing here, that they may believe that you sent me."

When he had said this, Jesus called in a loud voice, "Lazarus, come out!" The dead man came out, his hands and feet wrapped with strips of linen, and a cloth around his face.

Jesus said to them, "Take off the grave clothes and let him go."

Therefore many of the Jews who had come to visit Mary, and had seen what Jesus did, believed in him. But some of them went to the Pharisees and told them what Jesus had done. Then the chief priests and the Pharisees called a meeting of the Sanhedrin ... So from that day on they plotted to take his life.

Therefore Jesus no longer moved about publicly among the people of Judea. Instead he withdrew to a region near the wilderness, to a village called Ephraim, where he stayed with his disciples.

—John 11:1–47, 53–54 NIV 2011

WALKING IT OUT

'Tis the look that melted Peter,
'Tis the face that Stephen saw,
'Tis the heart that wept with Mary,
Can alone from idols draw.

In *Revise Us Again*, I made the statement that as high as God is going to elevate you is as deep as He digs to lay the foundation.

Sometimes the brightest light comes from the darkest places. And what doesn't destroy you ends up defining you in some significant way.

These truths boldly emerge in this narrative.

The raising of Lazarus from the dead is regarded by many Bible students as the crowning gem of Jesus' miracles, the climax of the seven signs of John's gospel.

The raising of Lazarus also foreshadowed the Lord's own resurrection, which was close at hand.

Interestingly, Lazarus is the shortened form of a name that means "God helps."

We don't know what Lazarus' illness was. Since it's not named, it was probably unremarkable. Common terminal diseases in the ancient world were scabies, smallpox, tuberculosis, various eye diseases (ophthalmos), dysentery, leprosy, and malaria.

Some scholars speculate that Lazarus was inflicted with the eastern fever.

In John 11, we are told that Jesus *loved* Martha, Mary, and Lazarus, and that they were His friends.[1]

In John 15:15, the Lord said to His disciples, "I no longer call you servants, because a servant does not know his master's business. Instead, I have called you friends, for everything that I learned from my Father I have made known to you."

Love and friendship. These two words sum up the heart of Bethany.

Bethany is the place where Jesus loves His own, and His own love Him. It is also a place of friendship ... friendship with the living God.

Jesus desires friends, not servants. He desires love, not servitude.

In the cold temple of Jerusalem, God was merely served. But in the warmth of the Bethany home, He was befriended and cherished.

When I read John 11, I see a Lord who is saying, "I didn't come to this earth to be served. I came to have friends. I came to love and be loved. I came to take a people into My heart. I came to unveil the secrets of My heart to My friends."

But what do love and friendship look like according to Jesus?

Think about this: Jesus allowed Lazarus to suffer illness. He allowed Mary and Martha to experience the agony of watching their brother fade away.

Even worse, Jesus allowed Lazarus to die. And in so doing, He allowed two precious women to lose their only brother.

And all the while, Jesus loved Lazarus, Mary, and Martha and regarded them as His friends.

Keep this in mind the next time you get sick, lose a loved one, or face a crisis or tragedy.

The Lord allows painful things to happen to those He loves. He allows tragedy to befall His friends. Yet He loves you while you're sick. And He loves you even after you die.

Death in Bethany

John painted the scene with graphic interest. Here is Bethany, the only place on earth that the Lord could feel at home. And tragically, the sweet oasis of Bethany is disrupted by death. Bethany, as Jesus knew it, had come to an end.

Lazarus died.

When Jesus became aware of this, He was master of the situation. He was in complete control, free of worry and hurry. He heard from His Father on the situation and obeyed His leading. Even though He was visibly disturbed, there was no tremor in His voice.

It was dangerous for Jesus to return to Judea because of the fatal fury of the Jews. Judea's death squads had recently tried to kill Him. So He lingered by the Jordan.

Perhaps that's why Mary and Martha were reluctant to call for Him. Yet they eventually sent Him a message informing Him of their brother's sickness.

When Jesus approached the village, Martha acted according to character. She ran impulsively to see Him, almost chiding Him for not coming sooner.

Mary also acted according to character. When she came into the presence of Christ, she fell at His feet and began to weep.

The scene was chaotic, the air thick with grief. Mourning and sorrow were everywhere. A chorus of women from Bethany and nearby Jerusalem bemoaned the death of Lazarus. God's greatest enemy had taken the one whom Jesus loved.

So there was death in Bethany. But there was also resurrection.

In resurrection, God starts all over with a new creation. But resurrection always follows suffering and death.

Herein lies an important lesson. If you make a home for the Lord Jesus Christ, hard times will come. Crisis will come. Suffering will come. Even death—*in some form*—will come.

Suffering is worldwide and neck deep. But for the Christian, suffering has a special purpose. It's the chiseling of God designed to transform you into the image of His Son.

Information doesn't produce transformation. Suffering that leads us to embrace Christ does.

Imagine a strong-willed Christian in his early thirties. We'll call him Jeff. Jeff is naturally gifted to preach. People follow him easily. He is strong in himself, opinionated, quick to answer. But though he speaks powerfully, you don't sense Christ from him.

Jeff is serving God with all burners cranked on high. Through various circumstances, God brings a crisis into his life, one that causes him to become unglued. The gears come to a halt. God stops him cold, and Jeff is left sucking air. The Lord knows exactly how to take the wind out of our sails to slow us down.

Jeff has just met a God who he thought he understood. However, the Lord is suddenly elusive, and Jeff finds himself reeling for a while. He feels stuck. Limited. Confused. Frustrated.

Jeff puts his ministry on hold. In his confusion, he begins to seek the Lord, and he also receives counsel from an older believer seasoned in suffering.

Several years pass, and the cloud lifts. Jeff is different. He's not so quick to answer. He's less sure, less opinionated. But when he speaks, you sense the Lord. You touch the life of Jesus Christ.

What happened? There's been a resurrection, and with it, some transformation.

Chisel it in stone: you can't have a resurrection without a death. And you can't know the transforming triumph of Christ without a crisis. You can't know the hills without the valleys, and you can't make a sailor with calm seas. We easily forget this when we're going through the northeast corner of hell.

A word of encouragement: if your foundations are in Jesus Christ, then you can weather the storm. You can endure the crisis. You can put your asbestos suit on and walk through the fire because you are standing on Him who is the Immovable Rock.

Sometimes God will deliver you *from* trouble. Oftentimes He will deliver you *through* it.

Yet resurrection is always on the other side ... *if you stand and endure*.

A Spirit-led man or woman is someone who has faced tragedy, faced loss, looked unbearable and exquisite pain in the face ... and has stood his or her ground.

With their garments still smoking, these men and women have said before God, mortals, and angels: "It is well with my soul. God's enemy has thrown his best at me, and I'm still here. I'm still on the Rock. I've not sunk. I'm still standing. I've not been destroyed, and I've not gone under. I will continue to follow my Lord, come hell or high water. He is still on the throne!"

"Having done all, stand. Stand therefore" ... on the Rock that never moves.[2]

Be encouraged, dear child of God. If the Lord is with you, who can be against you?[3]

No matter how tight the screws get, you press on … by Him, through Him, and to Him.

As Winston Churchill once put it, "Success is not final, failure is not fatal: it is the courage to continue that counts."

The Tears of Jesus

When Mary spoke with Jesus outside the village, He was deeply troubled and disturbed. The Greek word translated "troubled" or "agitated" in John 11:33 indicates indignation.

But what was Jesus angry about?

Some have suggested that He was angry at the unbelief of Mary, Martha, and the Jews who mourned Lazarus' death.

Maybe. But I find this difficult to believe.

Rather, I tend to think that Jesus was angry at death and what it does to His beloved. How it robs them of those whom they cherish. How it inflicts them with the unspeakable agonies of grief. How it thwarts love by taking those who are beloved.

The tears of Jesus show us a God who is sensitive to our sorrows. Even though He knew He was going to raise Lazarus from the dead, He experienced the moment. Knowing that His soon-coming miracle would dry every eye, He wept nonetheless. He was deeply touched by the sorrow that afflicted Mary, Martha, and the whole village.

> For we have not an high priest which cannot be touched with the feeling of our infirmities; but was in all points tempted like as we are, yet without sin.[4]

Jesus, as it were, mingled His holy tears with theirs. Indeed, the Lord is able to "wipe away every tear" from our eyes because He Himself knows how to weep.

We read about the tears of Jesus three times in the New Testament:

His tears of sorrow over Jerusalem.[5]

His tears of suffering in the garden.[6]

His tears of sympathy in Bethany.[7]

Behold the tears of Christ. They teach us that our Lord is touched with the feeling of our infirmities. They teach us that He is not unmoved by our sorrow and suffering.

The Son of God wept aloud over the holy city, but He sobbed silently before the tomb of His friend.

These were the perfect tears of a perfect Man.

Know this: Jesus didn't relinquish His perfect humanity when He ascended far above the heavens. He still weeps with us today, for He is "the same yesterday, today, and forever."[8]

Consequently, He feels it when every heart burns, bleeds, or bends. He is a friend who "loves at all times."[9] Christ saves as the Son of God, but He feels as the Son of man. So in your hour of grief, remember: *your Lord is with you and feels for you.*

As Thomas Moore once put it, "Earth has no sorrow that Heaven cannot heal." Jesus is heaven personified.

It's interesting to contrast Martha with Mary in this story. What Martha said to the Lord was doctrinally correct.

> I know he will rise again in the resurrection at the last day... I believe that you are the Messiah, the Son of God, who is to come into the world.[10]

Her confession almost sounds like a creed.

By contrast, Mary fell at the Lord's feet and wept bitterly. And Jesus acted.

Martha didn't seem to understand that she stood in the presence of the One who wasn't just a great Teacher, but the Author of life.

While her almost creedal confession was doctrinally accurate, her doubt bled through when she protested after Jesus asked for the stone to be rolled away.

Jesus' words to Martha about His being the Resurrection and the Life evaporated before the reality of the tomb.

His response to her was telling: "Did I not tell you that if you believed, you would see the glory of God?"[11]

We cannot fault Martha. She's too much like us. Faith often takes a nosedive when we are on the brink of tragedy. At such times, we forget the Lord's words.

Sometimes confessions and creeds, as important as they are, are not enough to move God to act. Only falling at His feet and weeping will suffice.

At the same time, when we are standing on the raw, bleeding edge of tragedy, our spiritual instincts can become paralyzed. And the only thing that we can hold onto is our confession of faith. As Watchman Nee said, "The best prayer of all is not 'I want,' but 'Thou art.'"

Thou art the Christ, the Son of the living God.[12]

A God Who Waits Too Long

In our suffering, we want an explanation. But Jesus wants to give us a revelation … of Himself.

Every crisis in our lives is an opportunity to broaden, deepen, and heighten our revelation of Christ.

In Bethany, we discover a God who is willing to wait until it's too late.

Jesus showed up four days after Lazarus died. When the Lord received the message from Mary and Martha, He did not act. He deliberately stalled, waiting two days in Perea before heading off to Bethany.[13] Perea was where John the Baptist originally preached and baptized. It sat a little over twenty miles away from Bethany, a one-day journey.

Take note. Jesus rarely responds on a human level or in a way that fits human expectations. But He always acts according to His Father's clock.

While Jesus' delay appears cold and callous at first blush, it was simply a response to the Father's direction rather than a response to the human pressure to meet an external need. All who put their hands to the plow of God's work would be wise to remember this principle.

Jesus' deliberate delay did not suggest that He didn't love the Bethany family. John was careful to repeat how much Christ loved Martha, Mary, and Lazarus.[14]

Indeed, Jesus ultimately met the need. He just did it in a way that no one expected, which is a common characteristic of our Lord.

Look carefully at Jesus' prayer:

> Then Jesus looked up and said, "Father, I thank you that
> you have heard me. I knew that you always hear me, but I
> said this for the benefit of the people standing here, that
> they may believe that you sent me."[15]

These words give us insight into Jesus' prayer life. Most of His praying was internal. In this particular case, Jesus prayed aloud so the crowd would hear Him and watch the spectacular miracle that followed.

I've spoken about the Lord's internal fellowship with His Father elsewhere,[16] but it's worth noting here. And it leads us to a larger truth.

In 1 Corinthians, Paul said that the work of God can be accomplished by gold, silver, precious stone, or wood, hay, and stubble.[17] The difference is in the weight. Gold, silver, and precious stones are heavy and imperishable. Wood, hay, and stubble are light, inexpensive, and burn up quickly.

A great deal of Christian work today is wood, hay, and stubble. The engine that drives it is human need and wisdom.

Ishmael was the result of Abraham's impatience. Abraham grew tired of waiting on God. So he exerted his own strength, wisdom, and resources to produce a child.

But Ishmael wasn't God's choice. Isaac, who came much later, was the divine choice. And Isaac was born according to the principle of resurrection, when Abraham's body was "as good as dead" and Sarah's womb was dead as well.

Isaac was the result of God's action. To have God work in and through us will always trump human striving and labor.

In short, God must originate His own work. He must govern its end (and it must be to His glory). Finally, He must be the One who accomplishes it.

> For from him and through him and to him are all things.
> To him be the glory forever! Amen.[18]

Notice that it's not just "from Him" and "to Him." It is also "through Him."

To put it in memoir form: first I learned how to work for God. Then I learned how to work with God. Finally, I learned how to watch God work.

These truths are rarely discussed today among those who specialize in equipping Christians for ministry.

Ever since I can remember, I've known a God who seems to have the disturbing habit of leaving the scene when I most needed Him. When things got rough, He would often disappear.

At least that's how it seemed.

The Lord will not always rescue you when you want Him to. And He certainly will not act according to your timetable every time.

Sometimes He will let you die. In fact, He may wait until you're quadruply dead and stinking in your tomb before He does anything.

So when things become black in your life, and there seems to be no way out, your situation has the fingerprints of Jesus Christ all over it.

Death is invincible. It's also hopeless. But four days after death is *beyond* hopeless.

Lazarus' death was beyond human ability and aid. Only the living God could do anything about it.

There was a Jewish belief that the human soul remains near the grave of the deceased for three days, hoping to be able to return to the body. On the fourth day, however, the soul leaves the body permanently.

If the first-century Jews believed this, then the only hope of Lazarus' recovery was an act of God's power.

Mark it down: Jesus Christ will sometimes wait until you are long dead. But then … when you least expect it … He will come leaping over the hills in some strange and unforeseen way to do what you never dreamed.

Yes, God will allow you to get into situations that are beyond human aid. And at such times, His grace will not be sufficient. All evidence points to this at least. Why? *So that He might display the glory of His resurrection life.*

Resurrection is God's act alone. And that's why it always brings glory to Him.

So there was a crisis in Bethany. There was sorrow and suffering, even death. But there was also a resurrection. And the Lord cannot dispense the latter until we are willing to embrace the former. This is written in the very bloodstream of God.

The power of His resurrection always follows the fellowship of His sufferings.

Never forget: Jesus Christ is Resurrection, and He is Life. And if you outwait Him, He'll eventually roll the stone away and raise you from the dead.

While death is mighty, Jesus is Almighty. And His shocking and surprising presence will often make its appearance when you least expect it.

But that's not all.

Freedom from Bondage

It was a heart-stopping moment. The One who created the universe wept at the grave of His friend. And He, the Resurrection and the Life, raised him to life again. The words of Jesus in John 11:44 throb with majestic grandeur:

> "Loose him, and let him go."[19]

> "Free him, and let him go."[20]

> "Unbind him, and let him go."[21]

What is this? It's freedom from bondage.

I want to blow this story up so you can see it. Let's go back to the stirring drama and watch the scene unfold.

Look at the lifeless body of Lazarus. He's not just dead; he is rotting.

Jesus is looking straight at a sealed tomb. Perhaps the Father said to Him, "My Son, You too will be placed in a sealed tomb just like this one. And I will raise You up with the sound of My voice."

Surrounded by death, sorrow, wailing, mourning, and grief, Jesus doesn't get flustered. He is the unshakable Rock, immovable and confident in His God. He faces His greatest enemy without fear.

The Lord stands before the great maw of death. He approaches Lazarus' tomb prepared for battle, squaring off with death, the child of sin.

Jesus shouts. By His word, He dispenses His resurrection life and disarms the grip of death that held His friend for four long days.

Wielding only three words—"Lazarus, come forth"— Jesus turns the evening of mourning into the sunshine of joy. Lazarus is made alive—a new creature—free from the bondage of graveclothes.

The facets of death are many: spiritual blindness, spiritual deafness, darkness, inactivity, limitation, condemnation, etc. And death always brings bondage.[22]

Lazarus is tied hand and foot with burial clothes, and his face is wrapped in a cloth. He cannot see, hear, speak, or walk. He is in bondage.

But the Christ of God meets and overcomes death in all of its forms with life. He is death's Destroyer. And after bringing His friend back to the living, He thunders to the crowd, "Unbind him, and let him go!"

I see two things here.

First, Bethany is the place where God's people are set free from bondage. Bondage to dead religion, bondage to legalism, bondage to sin, bondage to the world, bondage to guilt and shame, bondage to the flesh, bondage to the curse of the Law, and every other kind of bondage.

> It is for freedom that Christ has set us free. Stand firm, then, and do not let yourselves be burdened again by a yoke of slavery.[23]

> Now the Lord is the Spirit, and where the Spirit of the Lord is, there is freedom.[24]

> You have been set free from sin and have become slaves to righteousness.[25]

> The creation itself will be liberated from its bondage to decay and brought into the glorious freedom of the children of God.[26]

> So if the Son sets you free, you will be free indeed.[27]

One of the most debilitating forms of bondage that a Christian can know is the bondage of guilt. It's paralyzing, depressing … devastating even. But Jesus Christ has removed your guilt. The blood of Christ is enough to satisfy a holy God and that blood looms larger in His eyes than any sin you or I can ever commit.

For this reason, your righteousness is not based on what you have or haven't done. It is solely based on what He has done.

So stand in the shed blood of Christ, which has cleansed you from sin, made you acceptable to God, and given you access to His "throne of grace." It is the accuser of the brethren who would seek to paralyze you with the gripping power of guilt. But we "[overcome] him by the blood of the Lamb."[28]

Indeed, there is freedom in Bethany, and it is the freedom that only Jesus Christ can bring.

Second, Jesus did not unbind Lazarus; instead He told the crowd to do it. It was as if He said, "I want you to co-labor with Me in bringing freedom to others. Since I have set you free, you are now My agents to set others free. I've called you to be My bondage-breakers for others."

"Loose him, and let him go!" is what the Lord said to those in Bethany.

If the Lord has set you free, He has granted you the power to set others free.

Note that Lazarus could not unbind himself. He needed others to do it. We cannot free ourselves.

This is precisely what resurrection life does. Resurrection life liberates us from all things except Christ Himself. And He gives us His resurrection life so that we may "go and do like-wise," liberating others from sin, condemnation, guilt, shame, the world, and the Devil.

Setting people free from bondage is deeply embedded in the soundtrack of Jesus' ministry.[29] And it should be embedded in ours as well.

This isn't a burden, but a glorious privilege.

The Lord's shout to an entombed Lazarus was a signpost of the last day when He will shout again:

> I tell you the truth, a time is coming and has now come when the dead will hear the voice of the Son of God and those who hear will live.[30]

> For a time is coming when all who are in their graves will hear his voice.[31]

The Lord's word to the disciples that Lazarus was asleep is more than a figure of speech.[32] According to the New Testament, Christians will never taste real death.

> I tell you the truth, if anyone keeps my word, he will never see death.[33]

GOD'S FAVORITE PLACE ON EARTH

Whoever lives and believes in me will never die.[34]

The sting of death has been removed from the believer.[35] So we do not die; we merely sleep. And Jesus will wake us up at the resurrection:

> After he had said this, he went on to tell them, "Our friend Lazarus has fallen asleep; but I am going there to wake him up."[36]

> Then he [Stephen] fell on his knees and cried out, "Lord, do not hold this sin against them." When he had said this, he fell asleep.[37]

> That is why many among you are weak and sick, and a number of you have fallen asleep.[38]

> But Christ has indeed been raised from the dead, the firstfruits of those who have fallen asleep.[39]

> Brothers, we do not want you to be ignorant about those who fall asleep, or to grieve like the rest of men, who have no hope. We believe that Jesus died and rose again and so we believe that God will bring with Jesus those who have fallen asleep in him.[40]

He died for us so that, whether we are awake or asleep, we may live together with him.[41]

According to John 10:24, the Jews gathered around Jesus and asked Him,

How long will you keep us in suspense? If you are the Christ, tell us plainly.

The Lord's monumental demonstration of divine power and glory, which raised Lazarus from the dead, was His answer to their query.

The raising of Lazarus from the dead was the precursor to His ultimate bout with death on a hill outside of Jerusalem. It was the opening act before the final act, which was the resurrection of Christ Himself.

One of the main themes of John's gospel is Christ as Life. For John, Jesus is the God of life who has come to turn a death-infested world upside down.

You can see this throughout Jesus' entire ministry. Wherever He went, He destroyed death in all of its forms.

The rulers of this world know death to be their greatest instrument. This is why they plotted to kill both Jesus and Lazarus (a living witness to Jesus' miraculous power). Thus the reign of God is about the Author of life breaking into and overcoming this death-filled world.

In Lazarus' resurrection, Jesus demonstrated that death no longer has the last word. Resurrection brings the gospel to its highest pitch. The beauty of the Christian message is that we have been given the risen life of Jesus to live by here and now.

Like Lazarus, the human race is sick and dying. On its own, it is helpless and hopeless. It's lying inside a tomb, lifeless and decaying.

But God desires to raise humanity from the iron grip of death, raising it from the tomb to new life and new creation. His will is to bring us out of the condemnation of death into resurrection peace and the power of an endless life.

This is what the gospel affords all who believe.

Jesus' words to Martha in this story are loaded. He was essentially saying, "Hope is nearer than you think. The last day has already arrived. I am the Resurrection and the Life."

That is the glorious edge of the gospel. In Jesus Christ, the life of tomorrow is available today.

And the challenge of Jesus to Martha is what He says to all of us today: *"Do you believe this?"*

The Forgotten Beatitude

In Matthew 11:6, Jesus said, "Blessed is the one who is not offended by me."[42] To be offended here means to stumble or trip. While Martha was probably tempted to take offense at Jesus, she eventually overcame her struggle.

Consider her words: "Lord, if You only had been here, my brother would not have died."[43]

Listen to that statement and think about her words.

"Lord, if You only had stepped in, then this terrorist attack wouldn't have occurred."

"Lord, if You only had stepped in, then my loved one wouldn't have gotten sick."

"Lord, if You only had stepped in, then this tsunami wouldn't have taken place."

"Lord, if You only had stepped in, then [fill in the blank] wouldn't have happened."

"Lord, if You only had …"

Have you ever bemoaned an event in this way? If you have a pulse, you no doubt have.

Martha had three reasons to be offended by her Lord.

First, Jesus did not arrive in time to heal Lazarus. Second, Jesus' words to the messenger could easily have been interpreted to mean that Lazarus would not die. Third, Jesus did not show up for Lazarus' funeral. In the first century, those who died were buried immediately. Six days of mourning followed. If close friends were not in attendance during the burial, it brought shame upon the family and the deceased.

Martha may have also felt slighted when Jesus asked for Mary after He arrived in Bethany. Perhaps she thought to herself, *It doesn't matter what I do or say, it's always about Mary!*

Regardless, being offended by the Lord is something that touches us all.

The Scripture tells us that Jesus is a rock of offense to the disobedient.[44] In His earthly days, Christ was constantly offending the outwardly religious.

But when Jesus spoke these words in Matthew 11:6—"Blessed is the one who is not offended by me"—He had someone else in mind. He was speaking to His followers: "Blessed are you, My followers, when you are not offended by Me."

John the Baptist was utterly loyal to Jesus. He walked a life of total self-denial, giving up everything for his God. And then he found himself in a cold prison.

We have no record that the Lord ever visited John in prison. So John questioned and doubted. He was probably thinking,

Was it really worth it? I lived my whole life to pave the way for the Messiah, and now I'm in prison. The kingdom hasn't yet come. Did I miss it?

John wondered and wavered; he was tempted to be offended by his Lord. So he sent word to Jesus, asking, "Are you really the One who was to come? Or should we expect another?"[45]

Jesus didn't visit John. He instead sent an answer through John's disciples:

> Go back and report to John what you're seeing. The deaf hear; the blind see; the lepers are cleansed; the dead are raised; the good news is being preached to the poor … and happy is the person who is not offended in Me. Peaceful is the man who doesn't stumble over Me. Blessed is the person who doesn't fall away on account of what I do or not do.[46]

Over the years, I've watched Christians take offense with the Lord. Some of them passionately followed Jesus in their youth, only to renounce Him later. Why? They took offense, because they chose to be offended.

"Blessed is the one who is not offended by Me." This is the forgotten beatitude.

What follows are three reasons why Christians become offended by their God:

(1) He demands too much

In John 16:1, Jesus told His disciples that He was sharing "all these things"[47] so they wouldn't be offended by Him. Some of those "things" were stern warnings that they would be hated by the world and persecuted.[48]

The Lord made clear that following Him wouldn't lead to a bed of roses. Suffering and loss are involved. He promised thorns.

Unfortunately, some people today present a gospel that leaves the hard parts out. The result: Christians get offended when they realize what they've gotten into.

But Jesus lets us know up front what following Him entails. Even in His own day, some of His followers stopped walking with Him because they considered the cost too high.[49]

(2) He doesn't meet our expectations

The Lord often works in ways that we don't understand. I've heard some Christians say, "My life would have been much better today if I didn't follow Jesus in my youth. Look where it's gotten me."

In my book *Finding Organic Church*, I wrote about the Catch-30 crisis. There comes a point in all our lives where we reassess the major commitments we've made in early adulthood. And we either dig in deeper or we detrain.

Isaiah says that God's ways are higher than ours.[50] The Lord works on levels that we cannot fathom. But He works all things for our good.[51]

"Why hasn't God answered this prayer? Why didn't He fulfill this promise? Why did He let this happen to me? Why did He let this happen to him or her? Why is God silent when I need to hear Him most?"

These are the questions that plague the mind of the serious believer.

If you've not yet met the God who refuses to meet all your expectations, you will. And how you react in that day will reveal whether you are worshipping Jesus Christ or Santa Claus.[52] It will show whether or not you love God more than His promises (or your *interpretation* of those promises).

Job said, "Should we accept only good things from the hand of God and never anything bad?"[53]

Would you still serve the Lord if it sent you to hell?

Recall the three Hebrew children. They lived lives loyal to their God. And the pagan king gave them an ultimatum: "Worship the golden image or else you're going to die in my fiery furnace."[54]

Their answer is telling: "We're not going to serve your gods or worship the image. The Lord is able to deliver us from your furnace and *He will deliver us*. But even if He doesn't, we still will not bow the knee to your gods."[55]

What attitude. What posture. What faith. "God will deliver us. But even if *He* doesn't, we will *still* follow Him."

Those words contain thunder and lightning for every child of God.

If I can use an illustration, we mortals are living on pages 300 to 400 of a 2,000-page book. Only God can see the whole book—the entire story. And He has given us the ability to see only pages 300 to 400.

We have no capacity to understand what's on pages 1 to 299 or pages 401 to 2,000. We can only speculate and assume what's in them. Hence we create all sorts of intricate theological systems to explain mysteries we don't understand.

The Lord doesn't show us all His plot twists. So life comes down to trusting in the Lord rather than trying to figure out His ways through our finite, limited understanding.

Yet with one another, we can better discover and understand what's in pages 300 to 400 and thereby learn to live more effectively within them.

Mary of Bethany didn't understand why Jesus didn't come to heal Lazarus. But she trusted Him nonetheless. Let us learn how to trust a God we don't fully understand.

(3) He doesn't show up on time

The story of Lazarus teaches us this in spades. The Lord works too slowly. He reacts too late. His deliverance takes too long. His clock seems defective.

We can text or email our prayer to God, and He doesn't text or email back when we expect. In fact, sometimes we never hear back from Him at all. The screen is blank.

Sometimes we'll pray for an important matter in our own lives … or we'll pray for someone else … *for years*. And the dial doesn't move.

Waiting on the Lord can become exhausting. And it can lead to offense. But God always keeps perfect time.

To sum up, here's how *not* to be offended by the Lord:

Remember that He demands everything, and He has promised suffering and tribulation along with blessing and eternal life. So don't sell out for a cheap, easy gospel. Such is not the gospel of Jesus Christ. He told us what we were getting into and exhorted us to count the cost ahead of time.[56]

Remember that His ways are higher than ours, and He doesn't always show us what He's doing or why. We may not always understand what He does or allows, but He can still be trusted. This is the nature of walking by faith rather than by sight. Even when His grace is not sufficient, when we look back, we realize that it was always sufficient.

Remember that God is always on time, but His clock ticks differently from ours. He's a Lord who sometimes shows up long after the hour of healing has passed and we have been dead four days. Just ask Lazarus.

Being offended by God is a choice. You can choose to take offense at the Lord and stumble over that which you don't understand. Or you can "trust in the LORD with all your heart, and lean not unto your own understanding."[57]

Basing your faith on God's performance—what you think He *should* do according to what you've been taught about His promises—is a profound mistake. Countless Christians have fallen away from the Lord when He didn't appear to fulfill His promises. Thus the only solid basis for an unwavering faith and an unshakable devotion is to believe that God *is* … and that He does "all things well," no matter what takes place.[58]

A. W. Tozer was correct when he wrote, "The worth of any journey can always be measured by the difficulties encountered along the way."

Jesus Christ is full of surprises. So much so that if Jesus isn't surprising you, then you've probably stopped growing in Him.

> O the depth of the riches both of the wisdom and knowledge of God! how unsearchable are his judgments, and his ways past finding out![59]

So Bethany is the place where mystery and majesty collide. It is the place where human power and hope come to their painful end.

It is the place where the immortal utterance of Jesus, "I am the Resurrection and the Life," is encountered in living color.

> Our friend Lazarus is sleeping, and I'm going to Bethany to wake him.[60]

It is the place where we discover that death doesn't have the last word. Jesus Christ does.

It is the place where God's people are made free from all forms of bondage.

It is the place where we encounter a God who doesn't meet our expectations but is touched with our sorrows and agonies.

It is the place where we are unoffended by a Lord who allows things to happen that we do not understand.

It is the place where God starts all over again with a new creation—a new life that's free from the bondage of death.

It is where we meet a persistent God who is determined to exalt His Son.

In all of these ways, the Lord desires for us to be a Bethany for His pleasure.

But there is something else still …

Chapter 4

ANOINTED IN BETHANY

Living after you have died is strange.

You appreciate life like never before. Martha's lentil soup never tasted so good. Even the capers, which I had never relished, were suddenly exquisite.

It had been months since Jesus brought me back to the realm of the living. And as was His custom, the Teacher visited us once again on His way to Jerusalem.

We did not know it at the time, but this visit would mark the last week of His earthly life.

That entire week, He would visit the holy city in the day and retreat in the evening to our home, where He and His disciples lodged overnight.

When we received word that Jesus was coming, my father decided to host a private dinner party to celebrate my resurrection. Jesus would be the guest of honor.

As usual, Martha served as hostess and Mary assisted.

Before the banquet began, Martha insisted that I sit next to Jesus, which I gladly did. My father sat at the head of the table with Jesus at his right hand in the place of honor.

Our house was packed to the brim that evening. Voices rose to the roof. Bright colors of clothing dotted the public room. Some of our closest friends were present, including relatives from Bethany and Jerusalem. It was a reunion of everyone we held dear.

The dinner party was held six days before Passover. And Jesus brought all of His disciples.

"Welcome!" my father boomed, greeting each person as they arrived. His eyes brightened with excitement. "You know my daughters, and you are in for a real feast tonight!"

Jesus complimented Martha's cooking as usual. "Your flatbread has no rival, Martha," said the Teacher.

Martha and Mary prepared an elaborate feast. A large plate of mixed meats was placed on the table. Another plate featured assorted vegetables with fish, turnips, beans, and a delicious brine sauce. Aged wine was also served.

We arranged two clusters of three couches around the table. Jesus, my father, some of the Teacher's disciples, and

I reclined around the low table, propping ourselves on cushions. The rest of the party sat on stools and benches in the open space in front of the table.

We all ate together, and Martha served.

Jesus was more solemn than usual that night. I kept watching Him while we ate, and He seemed to be deep in thought much of the time. His mouth pulled downward.

Near the end of the meal, I caught a whiff of an exotic scent. Others could smell it too, but none of us knew from where it came.

With dramatic suddenness, I looked down and saw my sister Mary kneeling at Jesus' feet. She snapped the narrow neck of a flask containing nard from India. The nard was an enormously expensive fragrance, worth the financial equivalent of three hundred days of labor.

Before her passing, my mother gave the nard to Mary as a gift. Mary was only seven years old then. One pound of the exotic perfume was sealed in a beautiful flask of alabaster. Candlelight flickered over the white jar.

I was shocked because this was Mary's future security.

The house fell silent as we fixed our gaze on Mary. What was she doing at Jesus' feet?

After breaking the fragile seal, Mary poured the nard on the Teacher's head. She did so liberally and profusely. So much so that it ran down His beard, droplets beading down over the fine hairs.

She removed His sandals and poured the rest of the nard on His feet, anointing them with it. She wiped them with her long black hair.

The immaculate head that would soon wear a crown of thorns was first crowned with the exquisite scent of my sister's perfume. Mary's flask of alabaster was the tangible token of the thankful outpouring and willing surrender of her heart.

The nard was, very simply, the most treasured possession she owned.

Mary had saved the nard for years. But the hour ripened for her to use it in a way that no mortal could predict.

I watched Jesus and a subtle smile streamed across His face. The fragrant beauty of Mary's act touched Him with quiet joy.

The Lord who had wept with my sisters at my tomb now rejoiced with us at our table.

The scent of the perfume, now completely exhausted on the Teacher, silently flooded the room.

The pleasant aroma matched the spiritual fragrance of my sister's act. And it left an indelible mark upon all of us. Especially Jesus.

Martha looked on with mild surprise. I saw tears running down her face as Mary anointed Jesus with the perfume.

At that moment, it dawned on me how much Martha had changed. She was still serving, but not anxiously. She was still hospitable, but no longer distracted. But even more than this, she had begun to understand the love that our sister had for the Teacher. And she affirmed it in her actions.

The sight of Mary unbinding her hair arrested the room. To those who did not understand what she was doing, it was a scandal. Some of our relatives glowered at her. Others recoiled in horror.

Embarrassment was written on the faces of some of the Teacher's disciples.

But to those who understood Mary, it was an act of extravagant love.

I glanced over at John. His eyes welled up with tears. The other disciples seemed irritated. A few of them turned their heads.

I have no words to adequately describe the sweetness of Mary's act that day. I knew my sister well, and she was motivated by the ardent love she had for the Teacher. It was a visible exhibit of unselfish worship and heartfelt devotion, a supreme tribute of her pure affection for Him.

None of us realized it at the time, but Mary outshined all the other disciples in her grasp of the Lord's worth as well as His imminent death.

Somehow she knew that the One who had raised me from the dead would soon take His own place in the tomb.

Years later I would reflect on this incident, remembering how Jesus would often tell us how He would be taken by the Gentiles and led to die. We did not understand what He was speaking about. But my sister, with her sensitive heart, understood.

❧

Weeks before, Jesus had consoled Mary in the hour of her grief. Now she consoled Him in the only way she knew how.

She anointed His head with the fragrant balm—the same way kings were anointed.

My father and I looked on with silent wonder and secret awe as Mary performed her beautiful act of devotion upon the Teacher.

Neither Jesus nor Mary spoke any words.

We quickly realized, however, that some of the Teacher's disciples did not have the same opinion.

Judas leveled a cold-hearted censure on my sister's act of worship:

"To what purpose was this waste? It could have been sold and given to the poor!" he chided.

I could hear some of the other disciples bristling in agreement with Judas' cutting criticism. They seemed infuriated. Mary's beautiful offering had been grossly misjudged.

When Judas finished, there was silence. Mary did not register an emotion. Her expression remained the same—her eyes still downcast.

Then, with quiet dignity, Jesus upbraided them all, saying,

"Leave her alone! Why are you troubling her? She has performed a good deed for Me."

Jesus paused. He looked at Mary and continued, "She has saved this perfume for the day of My burial. The poor will always be with you, and you can help them whenever you desire. But you won't always have Me. I tell you the truth, wherever in the world this gospel is proclaimed, what she has done today will also be rehearsed in her memory."

The Teacher knew exactly what Mary had done. Even beyond what she herself perceived.

In light of her beautiful act of worship, Jesus would allow no complaint. He would brook no criticism. Sharply and sternly, He defended my sister, openly rebuking the unjust charge.

Years later John told me that it wasn't Judas' care for the poor, but his greed that provoked his criticism that evening. Judas was the treasurer for the disciples, and the love of money had overtaken him.

But Judas' words betrayed him. He was a man with a cold heart and a closed hand. He did not recognize the worth of the Teacher, nor did he pay allegiance to Him.

His was the bitter complaint of a hypocrite.

Yet my sister's stunning act brought joy to the heart of the Savior. Even so, I could tell by her sad demeanor that Judas' remark cut her to the quick. But as was fitting for her character, Mary uttered no word in defense.

I was relieved when Jesus defended her. And I was honored when He said that her good deed would be remembered wherever the gospel would be proclaimed.

Shortly after Jesus finished speaking, a large crowd from Jerusalem arrived at our home. They heard that Jesus was visiting us, and they wanted to see Him (and me, whom He raised from the dead).

Our home smelled of the fragrance for days. When Mary poured the perfume upon the Teacher, some of it splashed on the table. And it even left a stain.

In the days to come, many of the Jews in Jerusalem believed in the Teacher because of the seismic miracle He performed on me.

But the chief priests, led by Caiaphas, were so threatened that they hatched a plot to put me to death. I was a living witness to the resurrection power of Jesus. The priests feared that if the Jews began believing in Him in larger numbers, the Romans would remove their established place in the city. So they wanted me dead to protect their real estate.[1]

My sisters and I scrambled to gather my belongings and pack them up. Under the cloak of darkness, I left Bethany in hiding. I went to Bethsaida in Galilee and stayed with the family of Philip—one of the Teacher's disciples.

Several weeks later, I received word that the Romans had put Jesus to death outside of Jerusalem, and I quickly made my way home.

The journey was long. The smell of donkey dung on the side of the roads filled my nostrils. My body was covered in gritty dust. Eventually, I rounded the corner, and our house in Bethany glimmered in the afternoon sun.

I staggered to the courtyard. Martha's hand stilled over her mixing bowl. "Lazarus!" she yelled.

My bags dropped to the floor. The sight of her calloused hands undid me. Tears burned my eyes. "They killed Him," she said.

I wrapped my arms around her. Our tears dripped to the ground.

In the days that followed, we could still smell the fragrance of Mary's perfume in the house. And whenever we looked at the stain on the table, we remembered.

We remembered all the times He visited our home and how He broke bread with us.

We remembered how Mary wiped His feet with her hair, anointing Him for His soon-approaching burial.

We remembered the many things He taught us before He visited the holy city one last time.

We remembered … and we wept.

But what happened next was the most surprising of all …

THE SACRED TEXT

Six days before the Passover Jesus came to Bethany, where Lazarus lived (the man whom Jesus raised from the dead). There at Bethany they prepared dinner for him at the home of Simon the leper. Martha was serving, and Lazarus was one of those eating with him.

Then Mary took an alabaster jar of expensive ointment (a pound of pure nard) and came up to him as he reclined at the table. She broke the jar and poured the ointment over his head. She anointed his feet and wiped his feet with her hair. The house soon was filled with the aroma of the ointment.

When his disciples saw what she did, [they] soon became indignant and said to themselves, "Why is this ointment being wasted? This could have been sold for a considerable amount of money." So they began to rebuke her. Judas Iscariot (who would later betray him) said, "Why wasn't this ointment sold for a year's wages, and the money given to the poor?" He didn't say this because he was at all concerned about the poor, but because he was a thief and had charge of the money pouch and kept stealing what was put into it.

Jesus was aware of all this and said to them, "Leave her alone. Why are you bothering the woman? She has done a good thing for me. She has saved this ointment for the day of my burial. You always have the poor with you and can help them whenever you want, but you won't always have me. She has done what she could. In pouring out this ointment she has anointed my body for burial. I tell you the truth, wherever in the world this good news is proclaimed, what this woman has done will also be recounted in memory of her."

Many of the Jews who knew he was there came not only because of Jesus but because they wanted to see Lazarus, whom Jesus had raised from the dead. That is why the chief priests discussed how they might also kill Lazarus. On account of him a large number of Jews were leaving them and believing in Jesus.

—Matt. 26:6–13, Mark 14:3–9, and John 12:1–11[2]

WALKING IT OUT

What has stripped the seeming beauty
From the idols of the earth?
Not a sense of right or duty,
But the sight of peerless worth.

In this story, we have a matchless picture of what Bethany is all about.

A banquet was given in honor of Jesus, and there was feasting, fellowship, and rejoicing. The banquet was set in the home of Simon the leper (which was also the home of Martha). Even though Simon no longer had leprosy, he still carried a stigma.

Yet Jesus received him.

God's house is made up of cleansed lepers. That's what we all are. We were inflicted with the dastardly disease of spiritual leprosy, an apt metaphor for sin. And Jesus Christ cleansed us.

> But you were cleansed; you were made holy; you were
> made right with God by calling on the name of the Lord
> Jesus Christ and by the Spirit of our God.[3]

Lazarus was also present—a resurrected man. God's house is made up of resurrected humans as well.

> Even when we were dead in our trespasses, [He] made us
> alive together with Christ ...[4]

Martha acted according to character. She was serving, but she was not worried or troubled as she had been before. Why? Because Martha was serving in resurrection.

Something had changed in her. You cannot be around Jesus Christ for very long without changing. His presence transforms.

In the past, Martha had served in her flesh. But on this night she served in the Spirit. She was not worried, troubled, or distracted. She served her Lord without complaint, without the need to be noticed or exonerated. She wasn't anxious about what others were doing or not doing. Her service was in proportion to her fellowship, and she was free.

Diligence is a wonderful trait. But it must go through death and resurrection for it to be properly adjusted and used by the Lord. This is what happened to Martha.

Mary also acted according to character. For the third time, she was at the Lord's feet.

She was at His feet in gladness, drinking in His words.[5] She was at His feet in sorrow, pouring out her grief.[6] And she was at His feet in worship, lavishing her love upon Him.[7]

Mary knew those feet well.

Put all of this together and step back. What do you see?

Cleansed lepers, resurrected humans, transformed servants, extravagant worshippers, brothers, sisters, fathers, and disciples all sitting around a table where Christ is the Head—feasting, fellowshipping, and rejoicing with Him.

That is Bethany!

Anointed for Burial

I want you to see the table. Jesus is reclining there.

Mary brings in a sealed flask of precious perfume. It's spikenard, an eastern perfume with a potent fragrance. It comes from the root of the nard plant found on the mountains of northern India.

It is obscenely expensive perfume, not oil—a luxury that few people could afford and enjoy in that day. Spikenard was used for burial rites as well as for cosmetic and romantic purposes. And it was virtually always used in small quantities.

Mary breaks open the seal and pours out the perfume upon the Lord's head, anointing Him as though He were a king. As the perfume drips down His body and reaches His feet, she anoints His feet with the perfume as though she is a slave and He is her master.

Jesus interprets the act as preparation for His burial, something very important to first-century Jews. He invites those in the room to view Mary's outrageous gesture as a symbolic embalming. She is anointing Him as one would a corpse.

Mary anointed Him for burial.

Anointing a dead body with spices and ointment was done in preparation for entombment. The perfume would conceal the smell of the decaying corpse. It was as if Mary understood that the Lord wouldn't be with them much longer, almost without realizing that she understood.

Mary perceived that her king was going to die. The kings of Judah were anointed before their coronations. Not by women, but by male prophets. In this case, Mary took on the role of a prophet.

Anointing a person's feet was also done to bring comfort and refreshment to them in a day when their feet were weary from travel. Mary's loving gesture of lowly devotion would comfort Jesus before His trial of pain.

The Unfathomable Worth of Christ

Consider the value of this perfume. It was worth three hundred denarii. A denarius was a day's wage for the average worker in the first century.[8] Three hundred denarii is one year's salary. Let me put this in contemporary terms so you can feel the force of it.

At the time of this writing, the average annual income in America is approximately fifty thousand dollars. So the value of that flask of perfume was the equivalent of fifty thousand dollars.

Mary probably received the perfume as a family heirloom. It represented her savings, her future, her security. It could have been sold in case of a financial crisis.

With that thought in mind, I'd like to make three observations about Mary's extravagant act:

(1) Mary recognized the supreme worth of the Lord Jesus

Mary took that which was most precious to her, and she gave it to her Lord. Not just some of it. But *all* of it. She poured the *entire* contents of the flask ... one Roman pound of undiluted nard ... upon Jesus. A Roman pound is close to twelve ounces.

I'm impressed that Mary saved this precious perfume for Christ. Even when her own brother died, she didn't use it for his burial. Instead, she kept it as a treasured gift for her Lord.

The shadow of the cross hovered over the banquet. By instinctive love and intuitive foresight, Mary knew that Jesus wasn't going to be with the family much longer. Thus her act was in perfect season.

It was an elegant picture of extravagant worship, extravagant loyalty, extravagant love, and extravagant devotion. And it was precious in the Lord's sight.

Jesus prized Mary's love and faith in a special way. He gave her act a deathless fame that would spread everywhere the gospel was preached. Her good work won His warmest praise, being rewarded with a renown that was beyond the legacy of kings. And in the face of abrasive criticism, Jesus defended and commended Mary with words of matchless beauty and tenderness.

Recall what Paul said in Philippians 3:8:

> I consider everything a loss compared to the surpassing greatness of knowing Christ Jesus my Lord, for whose sake I have lost all things. I consider them rubbish, that I may gain Christ.

In Bethany, Jesus Christ is valued for His exceeding worth. In Bethany, there is nothing too costly to lay at His feet. In Bethany, all things are counted as loss for the excellent knowledge of Christ Jesus our Lord.

But even more, the way that Mary anointed Jesus was scandalous. It was shameful for a woman to unbind her hair in public with men present. It denoted loose morals and was guaranteed to raise pious eyebrows.

Mary of Bethany's anointing shouldn't be confused with a previous anointing by a "sinful woman" in Luke 7. There are too many discrepancies to view it as the same event, including the location, the people involved, the way the anointing was done, and the time at which the event took place.

In addition, there is no evidence to suggest that Mary of Bethany was a sinful woman. Quite the contrary.

Perhaps Mary heard of the woman who had anointed Jesus in the past and was inspired by the idea. This is quite possible. (The post-apostolic Christians believed the sinful woman was Mary Magdalene, though this cannot be proven or disproven.)

Regardless of whether Mary heard about the previous anointing or not, she was taking a profound risk by unbinding her hair in public. A risk that demonstrated that she didn't care what others thought about her worship.

At bottom, Mary's stunning act wasn't motivated by the things that often govern spiritual service today, such as guilt, duty, obligation, the desire to impress others, the thrill of being appreciated, and the need to satisfy restlessness.

No, she performed this shameless gesture for an Audience of One. Her eyes had been opened to see the supreme value of Jesus Christ. And the Lord defended and commended her for it.

(2) Mary shattered the flask

The shattering of the alabaster flask signifies excessive use wherein nothing was saved. Once opened, the flask could not be resealed.

John wanted his readers to know that when the flask was broken, the house was filled with the aroma of the perfume. Herein lies a great spiritual principle:

When the vessel is broken, the fragrance of Christ pours forth.

This brings us back to the matter of brokenness that we discussed in chapter 1. The alabaster cruse was beautiful and expensive. But it had to be broken in order for the sweet perfume to be released and the scent enjoyed.

> But we have this treasure in jars of clay to show that this all-surpassing power is from God and not from us.[9]

Brokenness is a mark of the spiritual history of the Lord's choicest servants. Our lives can only become fragrant with the Lord's life when we've experienced the inner depths of brokenness. When something has been broken within us, something of God—who dwells in our spirits—is released, and the scent cannot be missed.

Charles Spurgeon rightly said that the jewels of the Christian are his or her afflictions. When people allow the Lord to break them and when they waste themselves upon Christ, those who come near them can sense the fragrance of His life.

There is nothing more precious on the face of this earth than a gathering of believers in whom the Lord feels at home.

Whenever that takes place, there is an issuing forth of the aroma of Christ's presence that can be detected by those who visit. It is the aroma of lives fully yielded to Jesus, poured out and wasted upon Him.

In the Messianic prophecy of Psalm 45, we are told that the Lord's garments smelled of myrrh and aloes. Before Jesus was buried, Nicodemus placed myrrh and aloes on His body. And he used the same amount that was used for royal burials—a hundred pounds worth.[10] By this act, Nicodemus testified that he believed Jesus to be a king.

Now think with me. In addition to the perfume that Mary poured upon Him, the Lord's body was covered with a hundred pounds of fragrant spices. So when He rose from the dead a few days later, He was fragrant. And His fragrance could be smelled from afar.

Point: *the resurrected Christ has a scent. He emits the everlasting fragrance of resurrection.*

Now we cannot physically smell Christ today, but our spiritual senses can detect the fragrance of His presence among us.

The house was filled with the fragrance of the perfume.[11]

The sense of smell is the most delicate of all the human senses. By it, we receive impressions beyond our sight and hearing. Fragrance cannot be hidden. It's pervasive. When released, the fragrant influence of Jesus Christ cannot be hidden.

> But thanks be to God, who always leads us in triumphal procession in Christ and through us spreads everywhere the fragrance of the knowledge of him. For we are to God the aroma of Christ among those who are being saved and those who are perishing.[12]

As A. B. Simpson once put it, "Preaching without spiritual aroma is like a rose without fragrance. We can only get the perfume by getting more of Christ."

(3) Mary was criticized by Judas

This story contains the only sermon that Judas ever preached. Listen to his three-word protest.

"Why this waste?"

When Judas saw Mary's worshipful act, he exploded with criticism, saying, "Why are you being so wasteful? You could have helped the poor with this small fortune!"

But Mary stepped out in faith. Her act of extravagant love was shameless, selfless, and risked both embarrassment and the sneers and jeers of harsh criticism.

But love compelled her.

However, her act was rudely interrupted by a mean-spirited complaint. Her token of exquisite devotion exposed her own heart and the heart of Judas as well as the other disciples who agreed with him.

Judas sought to cloak the real motive behind his complaint with pious rhetoric. It was a case of cold-heartedness judging warm-heartedness under the guise of being spiritual.

Unfortunately, Judas is not alone in engaging in this behavior.

There are few things that are as close to God's heart as helping the dispossessed and oppressed. Read your Old Testament. It's spilling over with God's concern for their plight.

Jesus Himself was a poor man all His life. The poor were His representatives, not His rivals.

But as important as caring for the poor is, Jesus Christ Himself is even more important. He is more valuable than any ministry, no matter how good or noble.

As we observed in chapter 1, it is possible to worship the god of "ministry" in place of Christ.

Interestingly, the Lord's death, which Mary highlighted by her anointing, would eventually solve the problem of poverty forever.

The contrast between Mary and Judas is dramatic. In Mary, we see the light of love. In Judas, we see the darkness of sin. Mary anointed Jesus for burial; Judas prepared Him for betrayal. Mary loved Christ in preparation for His death; Judas helped bring about His death.

I'm comforted to know that Jesus is an advocate to all who give Him the place of preeminence. He rises to the defense of every Mary.

While Mary was misunderstood and denigrated, she never justified, defended, or explained herself. Though she only speaks once in the Gospels, the legacy of her life speaks volumes by her actions.

For these reasons, Mary came closer to Jesus' inner heart than anyone else.

And her loving act is one case among several where a woman got it right while the men got it wrong.

Every disciple of Christ has much to learn from Mary.

Why This Waste?

What you give to Christ equals the measure of His worth in your eyes.

The worth of Jesus is immeasurable. It cannot be calculated. And nothing is too valuable for Him. Mary understood this.

Aware of the criticism that was leveled against her, Jesus said, "Why are you bothering this woman? She has done a beautiful thing to me."[13]

The Lord was simply saying, "I am worth far more than the value of this perfume. The poor will always be present, and you can help them whenever you desire. But you will not always have Me with you in the flesh."

> There will always be poor people in the land. Therefore
> I command you to be openhanded toward your brothers
> and toward the poor and needy in your land.[14]

What is waste? It is giving more than necessary. Waste is when you give a diamond to a dog. It is when you give something valuable to that which is inferior in worth. When something of value could be better spent elsewhere, we call it waste.

What Judas and the others were really saying was,

"The Lord isn't worth it."

Mark it down. Whenever you give that which is most valuable in your life to the Lord Jesus Christ, some of your fellow Christians will consider it to be waste.

"Why aren't you going to college to prepare for a career? Instead you foolishly chose to give your full attention and time with that group of Christians. Why are you wasting your youth?"

"Why did you break up with that person? They had a great job, and you could have had a wonderful future with them. You forfeited that relationship just because they weren't as 'religious' as you are. Why are you wasting your future?"

"Why did you sell your house and move to a smaller house simply to get involved with that ministry? Why are you wasting your money?"

"Why did you quit your job and relocate to be involved with that church? You now have a lower-paying job. Why are you wasting your life?"

"Why did you use your stock dividends for that work of God? Why are you wasting your savings?"

Whenever you hear the complaint, "Why this waste?" examine it carefully and consider whether you're hearing the gospel of Judas or not.

If you are, then the Lord's response where you are concerned is:

"Let him alone …"

"Let her alone …"

"He is doing a beautiful thing to Me."

"She is doing a beautiful thing to Me."

What some regard to be waste is beautiful in the Lord's eyes.

The truth is: *the only way to keep yourself from wasting your life is to waste it on Jesus Christ!*

Thus the answer to the question, "Why this waste?" is simply … "because Christ is worthy."

Watchman Nee once said that the Lord will never be satisfied without our "wasting" ourselves upon Him, and "real usefulness in the hand of God is measured in terms of waste…. [O]ur work for him springs out of our ministering to him."

Jesus was given costly gifts when He entered into this world.[15] And He was given a costly gift when He was about to exit it.[16] Today, He is still worthy of our best. And it is still costly to anoint the head of Christ.

I believe the Lord has His crosshairs sighted on something in all of our lives—whatever we hold dearest.

Your mind may immediately go to a person who has become a rival for your affections for Jesus. Or it may go to some vice that you know you need to abandon. But the more subtle competitors are actually spiritual things.

We've already mentioned that some make "Christian service" a god that competes with Jesus Christ. On that score, Henri Nouwen said that the main obstacle to love for God is service for God.

But another competitor is theology. It's possible to make theology our god instead of God Himself. We can love theology more than we love God.

The same is true for worship, believe it or not. It's possible to love the act of singing worship and praise songs to the Lord more than we love the Lord Himself.

It's possible to love arguing on behalf of God (apologetics), evangelizing for God, preaching about God, writing about God, and studying God (analyzing the Bible) more than loving God Himself.

All of these things are good, of course. But if they don't lead us to the real person of Christ, they can become idols.

If our hearts are awakened to discover the true worth of Jesus, we will be able to lay all things down at His feet. Herein lies the antidote to being a lukewarm Christian.

Our eyes must be opened to behold His peerless glory. Once that happens, we will realize that nothing is too good for Him, and we will break loose from our spiritual lethargy.

This, in fact, was Paul's great prayer in Ephesians. That God would grant to us "the spirit of wisdom and revelation in the knowledge of him."[17]

Many a preacher has tried to guilt God's people out of their lukewarm state, using shame, duty, and condemnation as instruments. But such tools are short-lived.

To see Christ with eyes not physical is the cure for spiritual apathy. So expose yourself to ministries that know how to preach Christ in such glory that you're awed by His greatness and you're drawn to worship Him. Our alabaster boxes willingly yield at the sight of His peerless worth.

As a friend of mine once said, "The moment He set me free is the moment He captured me."

The House of Figs

Mary anointed Jesus on a Saturday. On Sunday morning, He entered the city of Jerusalem, riding on a colt.[18] The Lamb of God presented Himself publicly in Zion as a humble king.

Before sundown that same day, He left Jerusalem and returned to Bethany, where He lodged.[19]

On Monday morning, He left for Jerusalem again. And on the way there, He hungered and saw a fig tree with leaves. Upon closer inspection, He discovered that there were no figs on it.[20] Here's what the text says:

As Jesus was returning to Jerusalem from Bethany the next morning, he became hungry. In the distance by the road he saw a fig tree covered with leaves, so he went to find fruit on it. When he reached it, he found only the leaves (it wasn't the right season for figs). So Jesus said to it, "May you bear no fruit from this time onward, and may no one ever eat your fruit again."

His disciples heard him say it. And the fig tree immediately withered. Then they came to Jerusalem, and Jesus went into the temple of God and began to drive out everyone who was selling and buying things there … Then he left them, and when the evening came he left the city and spent the night in Bethany. The next morning they passed by the fig tree and saw that it had dried up from the roots. Peter remembered and said to Jesus, "Master, look! The fig tree you cursed has shriveled up."[21]

A fig tree's leaves typically appear at the same time as its fruit. Thus to see a fig tree covered with leaves but no fruit meant that it was barren.

The tree in this story was a defective tree. And it was bearing a false testimony. It was announcing that it possessed figs (by the fact that it had leaves on it), while it had none. Jesus cursed it, and it withered away.

Note that the Lord didn't curse the fig tree because it was barren. He cursed it because it bore false witness.

The fig tree could not feed the Lord. It produced no figs, so it could not satisfy His heart.

But there was a place that could feed Him. There was a place that could satisfy His heart.

At sundown, Jesus returned to Bethany.[22]

And what happened in Bethany? Our Lord was fed. He was cared for. He was loved. And He was satisfied.

Ironically, Bethany means house of figs.

Many scholars agree that the fig tree represents Israel.[23] Like the fig tree that Jesus cursed, Israel put forth an outward show of religion. But in reality, it was spiritually barren. And it could not satisfy the heart of God.

Israel was supposed to feed our Lord, but it fed itself instead. The nation rejected its Messiah. "He came unto his own and his own received him not."[24] So He cursed the fig tree as an act of judgment, and He declared that it would never yield figs again.

In the Gospels, the cursing of the fig tree is mentioned with the cleansing of the temple. Both were signposts of God's judgment on Israel and its religion. Israel was like a barren tree, fruitless, and ripe for God's chastisement.

Each event—the cursing of the fig tree and the cleansing of the temple—contains the same message. Both were dramatic parables—symbolic actions—of divine displeasure and judgment.

Jesus cleansed the temple sometime after He cursed the fig tree, on Monday. On Tuesday, He went to Jerusalem to speak to the people for the last time. On Wednesday, He tarried in Bethany. On Thursday, He went to Jerusalem, ate the Passover in an upper room, and prayed in agony in the garden of Gethsemane. On Friday He was crucified.

Blessed Are the Unoffended

When Martha complained to Jesus about Mary on His first visit to Bethany, Mary could have chosen to be offended by her sister. But there is no indication that she felt that way. She also could have taken offense when Judas and the disciples protested against her act of extravagant worship. But again, there is no indication that she did.

Don't make the mistake of underestimating the pain that was inflicted upon Mary in both situations. Here was a woman who loved her Lord with all her heart, and she was unfairly criticized for it. Not by her enemies, but once by her sister and another time by some of the Lord's own disciples.

It reminds me of the old adage, "No good deed shall go unpunished."

The words of Elbert Hubbard come to mind: "To avoid criticism, do nothing, say nothing, and be nothing."

In both cases, Mary never opened her mouth to defend herself or her actions. In silence, she entrusted the matter to her Lord. And in both instances, Jesus rose to her defense.

Point: *there will always be some Christians who will undermine and denigrate your good actions.*

T. Austin-Sparks once wrote, "If you get upset, offended, and go off and sulk, and nurse your grievance, you will die."

With that in mind, here are eight things I've learned about being offended by others:

(1) Christians will hurt your feelings

Because of the fall, this will happen.[25] Sometimes a person acts with malicious intent, desiring to hurt you because they don't like you or they've *chosen* to be offended by you. Other times they will hurt you without realizing it. I'm sure that when the other disciples chimed in with Judas' complaint, they weren't trying to hurt Mary. It was just the result of fleshly judgment.

(2) When others hurt you, your spiritual maturity will be revealed

You will discover how real your relationship with Jesus Christ is when your feelings get hurt. You can be the greatest speaker, the greatest worshipper, or the greatest evangelist, but when your feelings are hurt, what you do at that moment and afterward will reveal the reality of your relationship with Jesus.

People have one of two reactions when their feelings get hurt: they deal with it before the Lord, or they destroy others. Mary left it in the hands of Christ.

(3) God intends to use mistreatments for our good

Recall the mistreatment that Joseph endured at the hands of his own brothers. Joseph took it from the hand of God, saying, "You intended to harm me, but God intended it for good."[26]

Remember King David when Abishai cursed him? David chose not to kill his detractor, but instead he saw the persecution in light of God's sovereign hand.[27]

To paraphrase Romans 8:28, everything that comes into our lives, whether good or evil, first passed through the hands of a sovereign, loving God before it got to us. And He uses it for our good.

Once you make peace with God's sovereignty and His ability to write straight with crooked lines, the more at peace you will be with those who mistreat you. While God is not the author of confusion or evil, He seeks to use all things for our transformation.

When Jesus defended Mary, He transformed her act into an immortal example of what real worship entails. Her example was such that we're still talking about it two thousand years later.

(4) Christians often get offended by reading into words and actions

This usually happens when a person is oversensitive and thin-skinned. In my experience, this makes up most cases in which a Christian takes offense at another believer.

As a group, Christians are the most easily offended people in the world when we should be the least. While Mary was mistreated twice, she didn't take offense.

(5) Christians often get offended with a person when they believe false accusations against them

Wise and discerning Christians who have been around the block ignore gossip that puts other believers in a bad light. In fact, in the eyes of the wise and discerning believer, any statement that has a defamatory tone is discredited out of the gate.

When wise and discerning believers are concerned about someone, they go straight to the person privately as Jesus taught us to do, asking questions rather than making allegations.

Some Christians, however, never think to do this. Instead, they readily believe slanderous allegations about a sister or brother in Christ without ever going to that person first.

The question "How would I want to be treated if someone were saying these things about me?" never seems to occur to them. The life of Jesus Christ always leads us to live that question. The flesh always leads us in the opposite direction.

Remember, Satan is the slanderer (that's what "Devil" means), and he uses gossip to destroy relationships. That's why the Bible says that believing gossip separates close friends[28] and that one of the seven things the Lord hates is "sowing seeds of discord among brethren."[29]

(6) What you do with a hurt is a choice you make

You can choose to be offended and make a friend out of your hurt, feed it, take it out for daily walks, cuddle it, and protect it until it destroys you and others. A root of bitterness, if allowed to live, will defile many and prove destructive to your own spirit.[30]

You can also choose to be offended and retaliate actively or passively.

Or you can choose to live by Christ and bring your hurt to God. Sometimes the Lord will lead you to go to the person and talk to them in a gracious manner, seeking reconciliation.[31]

Other times He will lead you to forebear it, take it to the cross, let it go, and move on. "A man's wisdom gives him patience; it is to his glory to overlook an offense."[32]

Sometimes He will show you that you've completely misinterpreted the actions of another.

In cases of repeated abuse, which I'm not addressing in this section, getting others involved is often wise and necessary. Forgiving someone doesn't mean you should enable that person to commit a crime or continue to devastate the lives of others.

(7) To be offended by a child of God is to be offended by God

When Jesus began preaching in His hometown of Nazareth, He offended His neighbors. They stumbled over Him and rejected who He really was.[33]

When you choose to take offense at another Christian, you are rejecting who they are in Christ. Thus it affects your relationship with Jesus, whether you realize it or not. Why? Because Christ and His body are connected, so "if you've done it to the least of these my brethren, you've done it unto Me."[34] Again, I'm not equating being offended with being hurt.

(8) You can live free from offense

This doesn't mean that you will never be hurt. Nor does it mean that you will never be angry. Jesus got angry. Remember His temple tantrum? Paul said, "Be angry and sin not. Don't let the sun go down on your wrath."[35]

Anger is a normal human emotion when someone abuses you or abuses someone you care about. But what you do with your anger determines whether or not it is sin.

In addition, we should always be "quick to listen, slow to speak and slow to become angry."[36] The Lord has called us to the high road of living without offense. And He has given us both the power and the will to do His good pleasure in this area.[37]

Remembering Mary

According to John's gospel, Jesus' ministry began with a banquet celebration, and it ended with a banquet celebration.[38]

What took place at the banquet in Bethany would be rehearsed everywhere the gospel would be proclaimed. Why? I cannot improve upon how this question was answered in one of my coauthored books:

> They beat Jesus' head with their hands, fracturing His nasal bones. They took turns spitting into the contusions of His blindfolded face and knelt before Him and taunted, "Hail, King of the Jews." Then they crushed onto His head that crown of thorns. With blood, spit, and sweat running down His face, Jesus looked around.
>
> Where were His disciples?
> Where were all His faithful followers?
> Where were all those whom He had healed?
> Where were all those whose eyes He had opened, whose ears He had unstopped, whose

mouths He had opened, whose limbs He had restored?

It was almost more than He could bear.

Then Jesus smelled the perfume ...

And when the soldiers beat Him with a whip until the blood ran down His back like a waterfall, His skin already supersensitive from the effects of hematidrosis (sweating blood); and when they marched Him 650 yards through the streets and made Him climb the Via Dolorosa, carrying the 150-pound patibulum on which His wrists were later to be nailed, reducing Him to a beast of burden being led to the slaughterhouse; when the weight of the cross produced contusions on the right shoulder and back on that three-hour walk through the city of Jerusalem to Golgotha on the Way of the Cross—He smelled the perfume.

And when they stripped Him naked and nailed Him to the crosspiece He had carried; when they took those six-inch spikes and lacerated the median nerves in His hands and feet; and when they lifted Him up on that cross, above the sinking garbage heap called Golgotha—Jesus smelled the perfume ...

And when everyone who passed by mocked Him on the cross; when the chief priests and scribes, even those thieves who were crucified with Him, taunted and teased Him in His agony; and when the loneliness became so severe He was about ready to call ten thousand angels to rescue Him, Jesus looked around. In the haze of hurt, He barely could make out the figures of the three Marys—His mother, Mary; His aunt Mary (wife of Cleopas); and Mary Magdalene—and then He smelled the perfume …

And when His body, already in shock, hung from the wrists, when He struggled for breath to chant two of His favorite psalms (31 and 22), unable to expel even small hiccups of sound without straightening His knees and raising Himself on the fulcrum of His nailed feet, the only thing the soldiers offered His parched throat ("I thirst!") so He could keep singing was a drink of vinegar, which only made singing more difficult … Jesus smelled the perfume.

And He remembered the woman who had given all she had so He would remember

> God's love for Him, and in that smell He could
> even detect the odors that reminded Him that
> He was going home, from whence He had
> come....[39]

John 11 closes with the chief priests plotting Lazarus' death. There is a principle here. Resurrection life will always provoke hostility, especially from the outwardly religious.

The Lord's Heartbeat

The Lord is looking for a group of people who will give Him first place in their lives, including their time. He's after a people who are willing to do whatever is necessary to satisfy His heart. In short, He's looking for a people who will love and worship Him extravagantly.

The gospel narrative of Bethany symbolizes all of these things.

God wants every Christian to be a Bethany, and He wants every church to be a Bethany—an extended family made up of sisters and brothers who waste themselves upon Jesus and satisfy His heart ... His very own "house of figs."

To this you and I have been called.

Let's now look at the fourth and final narrative ...

Chapter 5

ASCENDED IN BETHANY

After the icy hand of death laid me in a tomb for four days, the Teacher brought me back to life, giving me back to my sisters and father. In the same way, after Jesus suffered an intolerable death, the God of heaven brought Jesus back to life and gave Him back to all of us who loved Him.

Jesus raised me from the dead, so I should not have been surprised by this. But this time, Jesus was the One who died. I had no power to help Him. Everything seemed hopeless. And that is when His Father stepped in.

My sisters, my father, and I were privileged to see Him after He had risen. It is hard for me to describe. He looked different, yet He was the same and we knew it was Him.

Something strange had taken place … the Teacher, now resurrected.

My resurrection was to mortality; His was to immortality.

Conquering death once and for all, Jesus would never taste it again.

I will fall asleep again … soon I believe. But He will raise me up to immortality, giving me a glorious body just like His.

After He rose again, the Teacher spent forty days on the earth, appearing in different places to different disciples, teaching them about the kingdom of God.

When the time came for Him to leave us, He again visited my hometown, Bethany. It would be the last place that His feet would stand before He left us.

✦

A week before He left, word was sent to my family that Jesus wanted to meet us in Bethany.

Martha was in the courtyard when I heard her cry out. "Lazarus! Mary! You will not believe who is walking up the road!"

I lifted my head from my work and spotted Jesus striding toward us, followed by a large number of disciples. I expected Martha to heave her shoulders and march off to the kitchen, thinking, *So many people. So many mouths to feed*. Instead, she darted down the path to where Jesus walked.

I fetched Mary and my father. We ran to meet the Teacher with the others. Wonder swelled my chest. *What is He going to do?*

As we neared the outskirts of the village, Jesus stopped.

He spoke about the kingdom. At the time, we did not fully understand His words. But He told us that when the Spirit came, we would understand everything.

When He finished, He lifted His hands to the heavens and put them on each of our heads, one by one. We rested in the adoring wonder of the love of Christ as He blessed us.

I instinctively knew that whatever was happening, it was significant. The thought crossed my mind that I would not see Him again.

Many of us fell to our knees in worship.

But what I saw next stole my breath.

As we were on our knees, we lifted our eyes to Him. In that moment a cloud descended from heaven and enveloped Him.

And He began to slowly rise.

We watched as the dust fell off His feet while He ascended. Some of the disciples gasped. As He continued upward, His body cast an elongated shadow, touching the roots of a distant fig tree.

The cloud eventually took Him away from us, and He vanished from our sight. The eleven disciples stood to their feet.

Mesmerized by the strange sight, we all gazed into the sky where He disappeared. We then noticed two men standing beside us. They wore bright, shiny white robes.

The men addressed the eleven disciples, saying, "Men of Galilee, why are you standing looking up into heaven? This Jesus, who was taken up from you into heaven, will return in the same way that you saw Him ascend."

After saying these words, they disappeared.

Peter announced, "We are staying in the upper room in Jerusalem. The Lord instructed us to wait and pray for the coming of the Spirit. We would like to invite you all to join us there and to pray with us."

Everyone began to praise God. "Yes, yes, we will join you," some of us uttered.

Full of immeasurable joy, Mary, Martha, my father, and I went back to our home. We collected our belongings and met the others in Jerusalem to pray as Jesus instructed.

What happened ten days later is another story for another time. Suffice it to say that Jesus returned to us. But He returned in the form of the Spirit … to make His home inside of us.

When the Spirit came, each of us became a Bethany for the Teacher.

Everything that had taken place in the hamlet of Bethany was but a precursor for this life-changing event.

On that day—the day of Pentecost—we each became God's favorite place on earth … our own hearts and lives fashioned into a Bethany for the Lord.

THE SACRED TEXT

Then Jesus led them to Bethany, and lifting his hands to heaven, he blessed them. While he was blessing them, he left them and was taken up to heaven. So they worshiped him and then returned to Jerusalem filled with great joy. And they spent all of their time in the Temple, praising God (Luke 24:50-53 NLT).

So when they had come together, they asked him, "Lord, will you at this time restore the kingdom to Israel?" He said to them, "It is not for you to know times or seasons that the Father has fixed by his own authority. But you will receive power when the Holy Spirit has come upon you, and you will be my witnesses in Jerusalem and in all Judea and Samaria, and to the end of the earth." And when he had said these things, as they were looking on, he was lifted up, and a cloud took him out of their sight. And while they were gazing into heaven as he went, behold, two men stood by them in white robes, and said, "Men of Galilee, why do you stand looking into heaven? This Jesus, who was taken up from you into heaven, will come in the same way as you saw him go into heaven."

Then they returned to Jerusalem from the mount called Olivet, which is near Jerusalem, a Sabbath day's journey away. And when they had entered, they went up to the upper room, where they were staying, Peter and John and James and Andrew, Philip and Thomas, Bartholomew and Matthew, James the son of Alphaeus and Simon the Zealot and Judas the son of James. All these with one accord were devoting themselves to prayer, together with the women and Mary the mother of Jesus, and his brothers. In those days Peter stood up among the brothers (the company of persons was in all about 120).

—Acts 1:6-15 ESV

WALKING IT OUT

Idols once they won thee, charmed thee,
Lovely things of time and sense;
Gilded thus does sin disarm thee,
Honeyed lest thou turn thee thence.

Bethany was the last spot on earth touched by the feet of our Lord. From there, He said farewell to the world, until He descended in the Spirit on the day of Pentecost.

God's choices are always significant. He chose Bethany to be the place where women and men would see His face and hear the tone of His voice for the last time. He didn't choose Bethlehem, where He was born. He didn't choose Nazareth, where He grew up. He didn't choose Capernaum, where He set up His ministry center. Neither did He choose the holy city of Jerusalem, where God put His name.

He chose Bethany to be the soil that He last trod. Bethany— *His favorite place on earth*—the town where He was welcomed, loved, and worshipped during His short life. In Bethany, the heavens opened up to Him.

Looking over our narratives of Jesus in Bethany, we discover that there was a death in Bethany. There was a resurrection in Bethany. And there was an ascension in Bethany.

This reminds us of a profound truth: that our union with Christ brings us into the very experiences of Jesus Himself. For example:

- Our prayers to the Father through the Holy Spirit are Christ's prayers.[1]
- Our appeal to others on behalf of God is Christ's appeal to others.[2]
- Our affection for the members of the body is Christ's affection for the members.[3]
- Our deadness to sin is Christ's deadness to sin.[4]
- Our sufferings are Christ's sufferings.[5]
- Our burial of the old fleshly nature is Christ's burial.[6]
- Our spiritual resurrection is Christ's resurrection.[7]
- Our spiritual ascension is Christ's ascension.[8]
- Our spiritual glorification is Christ's glorification.[9]
- Our spiritual enthronement is Christ's enthronement.[10]

Those who are part of the body of Christ are completely and inseparably identified with, incorporated into, and eternally united with Jesus.

Thus His history is our history, and His destiny is our destiny. The key events that took place in Bethany remind us of this reality.

The Meaning of Ascension

Consider the atmosphere of the ascension. Jesus laid His hands upon His disciples and blessed them. This is how the high priest blessed the people of Israel. Here we have an image of Jesus stepping into His heavenly role of eternal High Priest.

> For this reason he had to be made like his brothers in every way, in order that he might become a merciful and faithful high priest in service to God, and that he might make atonement for the sins of the people.[11]

> Therefore, holy brothers, who share in the heavenly calling, fix your thoughts on Jesus, the apostle and high priest whom we confess.[12]

> Therefore, since we have a great high priest who has gone through the heavens, Jesus the Son of God, let us hold firmly to the faith we profess.[13]

Where Jesus, who went before us, has entered on our behalf. He has become a high priest forever, in the order of Melchizedek.[14]

Such a high priest meets our need—one who is holy, blameless, pure, set apart from sinners, exalted above the heavens.[15]

The point of what we are saying is this: We do have such a high priest, who sat down at the right hand of the throne of the Majesty in heaven.[16]

I believe that Mary, Martha, Lazarus, and Simon were among the 120 followers who were present at both the Lord's ascension in Bethany as well as the upper room on the day of Pentecost. We can deduce this by putting Luke 24 and Acts 1 together.

After the Lord was taken up into the heavens, His disciples were flooded with joy. And they continued to meet regularly in the temple courts to worship the living God. That is, they continued to be a Bethany for Christ on the earth.

Jesus Is on the Throne

The ascension of Jesus means that He is now on the throne. He has been crowned King of heaven and Lord of earth, sitting at the right hand of all power and majesty.

> After the Lord Jesus had spoken to them, he was taken up into heaven and he sat at the right hand of God.[17]

> The Son is the radiance of God's glory and the exact representation of his being, sustaining all things by his powerful word. After he had provided purification for sins, he sat down at the right hand of the Majesty in heaven.[18]

The resurrection of Jesus is the prototype of the new creation; His ascension enthroned Him as Lord of the world. His resurrection tells us that He is the beginning of the new creation; His ascension tells us that He is now in charge.

So no matter what befalls you in the way of disappointment, crisis, sorrow, or pain, remember: *Jesus of Nazareth is still on the throne.* And He is completely in control.

> Since, then, you have been raised with Christ, set your
> hearts on things above, where Christ is seated at the
> right hand of God.[19]

> Who is he that condemns? Christ Jesus, who died—more
> than that, who was raised to life—is at the right hand of
> God and is also interceding for us.[20]

Perhaps even more encouraging is the fact that when Christ ascended, He was enthroned as Head over all things. And all things were placed under His feet. Paul told us that we too ascended with Christ and we are also seated with Him in heavenly places.[21]

Christians aren't saved from troubles or delivered from problems. We have been given an ascendant life to rise above them.

If you take your place in Christ in heavenly places, your prayer life will change dramatically. No longer will you make beggarly requests for God to make you into something. Instead, you will pray from an enthroned position with Christ, declaring with thanksgiving what He has already made you in Himself.

"Lord, make me …" gives way to "Lord, You are … and I thank You that You have …"

We are seated in heavenly places in Christ. And since all things are under His feet, all things are under our feet as well.

It is our task to remind one another of this fact and believe it together.

All authority in heaven and earth has been given to our ascended Lord. And amazingly, He has given that authority to the church as well.[22]

Bethany, then, is the place of spiritual ascension.

The Drawing Power of Bethany

Immediately following the Lord's ascension, an angel announced that Jesus would return *in the same manner* in which He left.

The prophecy in Zechariah 14 seems to throw light on this statement:

> On that day his feet will stand on the Mount of Olives, east of Jerusalem, and the Mount of Olives will be split in two from east to west, forming a great valley, with half of the mountain moving north and half moving south.[23]

Remember, Bethany is located on the slopes of the Mount of Olives.

Could it be that when Jesus Christ returns to earth He will return to the very spot where He left? Could He return to *Bethany*, on the Mount of Olives? If so, would this not send a clear message that spiritual Bethanys are what the Lord is after and what will bring Him back?

I believe so.

Bethany possesses spiritual drawing power. When the Lord sees spiritual Bethanys all over the planet, He will return for His own because His own will receive Him. He will take over this planet as Head over all things, both in heaven and on earth.[24]

He will make the world a resting place for Himself—His dwelling.[25]

At the last sighting of the Lord on earth, the heavens opened above Bethany. Today, the heavens are still opened to a people whenever they choose to become a Bethany for Jesus Christ.

Just like in His earthly days, He will return to the place where He is fully received.

But there is one more point to consider …

Chapter 6

ANTICIPATING BETHANY

Bethany was priceless to the Teacher. It was priceless to Him because a certain family resided there, and I was privileged beyond measure to be part of that family.

Although Bethany was humble, obscure, and unpopular, Jesus chose my home to be His best-loved haven on earth. It was the only place where the Son of Man could lay His head. Bethany was an oasis for Christ in a world hostile toward Him. There He could pause, reflect, and find comfort and repose. It was a sanctuary of love and acceptance for the One who made all things.

As I reflect back on those precious times when we had Him in our home, I cannot help but think that Bethany possessed an irresistible charm for Him.

I am grateful that He spent His last week with us in the cherished seclusion of His favorite retreat—our tranquil home in Bethany.

❧

The earthly ministry of Jesus was profoundly short, but intense. The Teacher crammed countless years into three. It was toilsome and full of strain, excitement, and pressure.

His disciples shared in the wear and tear. I witnessed first-hand their frayed nerves, their fatigue, and the pain of being misunderstood, criticized, and attacked. They tread a lonely road.

In Bethany, Jesus and His first followers could find solace and rest. They would climb the brow of Olivet and lodge in our home, where my sisters prepared a warm meal for them. The village was a quiet and peaceful retreat away from the rigors of Jerusalem.

Bethany, and not Jerusalem, became the Lord's lodging place. Sadly, He could not spend a peaceful night in the holy city.

But in my village and in my home, He always found a warm welcome and caring hospitality. It was a lily among thorns. His place in a rejecting world.

For these reasons, I am grateful to have lived in Bethany. I was born here. And I will die here. I am honored to have been part of the Lord's favorite place on earth.

As I close, please remember the legacy of my sister Martha. It was to her, a woman, that the mystery of Jesus as the Resurrection and the Life was first disclosed. She served others until her final breath. She was a living portrait of the servant-hood of Jesus.

Remember the legacy of my sister Mary. Her beautiful act of anointing Him before His death has been narrated everywhere the gospel has been preached. Jesus wanted it this way because everywhere the gospel has taken root, the result should be "waste" in the way that my sister wasted herself upon Him.

I hope and pray that you too will be awakened to His supreme worth. For only then will you realize that nothing is too precious, nothing is too costly, and nothing is too valuable for Him.

And remember me, a living trophy to Jesus' power over death.

The day when He called me forth from the tomb will live in immortality. I am a breathing witness to His incomprehensible grandeur and unfathomable majesty.

The sound of His voice that woke me from death has never left me. And it will sound once again, waking all who believe in Him from their graves.

Regarding death, its power has been vanquished. So you have nothing to fear from it. I have been there before, and I came out on the other side … *alive and well.* And so will you.

Death's sting has been removed. So fear it not. I speak as one who was dead but now lives. Jesus now holds the keys of death and hades. It is safe to rest your head on a God who raises the dead.

I shall see Him again … soon. And I will rejoice to embrace Him another time, along with my loved ones who have gone before me.

As for you, my readers, take my story with you. Learn it and learn from it. And then live it.

Jesus is looking for a Bethany in every heart, every home, and every church.

So take the high ground and be a Bethany for the Savior.

He is worthy of nothing less.

Grace and peace,

—*Lazarus*

WALKING IT OUT

Draw and win and fill completely,
Till the cup o'erflow the brim;
What have we to do with idols
Who have companied with Him?

We have now come full circle. It was Bethany, and not Jerusalem, that Jesus chose to be His "safe house" on earth.

Bethany is forever linked to the crucial events of the Lord's life, particularly His last days.

In Bethany, we discover the reality of the Lord's teaching, the reality of His love, and the reality of His mission. It is there that we see the shadows of His death, resurrection, ascension, and second coming.

And when He comes back, where will He return? The same place from which He departed: *Bethany.*

The writer of Hebrews bids us to go to Him outside the camp of Jerusalem.

> So let us go out to him, outside the camp, and bear the disgrace he bore.[1]

If we are to go to Jesus, we must ask the question, where is He?

The answer. He is in Bethany … the place where He is received, appreciated, and enthroned.

For this reason, Bethany is always a reproach to the world, including the religious world. Bethany is not the place of crowds or popularity. Neither is it the place of the spiritually elite.

In the West, Christians envision the Christian faith to have a kind of spiritual upstairs reality. It's all about heaven and the future.

But Bethany is about today. It's about our vocation as we live for the Lord's rights between His first and second coming.

Bethany is a place for Christ in a rejecting world. A place that says, "Jesus is Lord of this earth, and we will make that fact a practical reality in a world where His rights are disputed, denied, and disowned."

Over the past few decades, entire movements have been built on Jesus' words to the rich young ruler to "sell all you have, give it to the poor, and follow Me."[2] Indeed, Jesus called the Twelve to leave their careers and follow Him. But He didn't issue this call to all of His disciples. The Bethany family is the summary witness to this fact. Martha, Mary, and Lazarus stayed in one place, and they were also well off.

Jesus never asked them to leave Bethany. Nor did He ask them to give away their possessions. Yet He regarded them as among His most intimate disciples and most beloved friends.

To be sure, consumerism is a spiritual snare, and the attachment to material wealth is the root of all kinds of evil.[3] But sharing what one has with others is what keeps our hearts detached from earthly treasures. This is the lesson that Mary, Martha, and Lazarus teach us.

To put it another way, it's not wrong to have material goods; it's wrong if material goods have us. And all things should be shared with those who have less.

Bethany gives us a living portrait of a theme that runs throughout the entire Bible. That theme is God's eternal quest for a home. In my book *From Eternity to Here*, I trace this theme from Genesis to Revelation.

The Bible opens with the Spirit of God "hovering" or "brooding" over the face of the deep.[4] There we discover that the Spirit was seeking a dwelling place for God, a place where He could commit His presence.

And from the tabernacle of Moses to the temple of Solomon to the tabernacle of David to the temple that Ezekiel saw in his vision, God has sought a home on this earth. Listen to His words through Isaiah the prophet:

> Heaven is my throne, and the earth is my footstool. Where is the house you will build for me? Where will my resting place be?[5]

Bethany represents the fulfillment of that prophetic cry. It represents the Lord's heart for every Christian and every church. God wants a Bethany in every city on this earth.

He wants a home.

A prophet is without honor in his own hometown. But Jesus Christ—*your Lord*—found a home in Bethany.

Consequently, the earth awaits a group of Christians in every city who will receive Him again utterly and completely:

A group of followers who will enthrone Christ as absolute Lord over their lives.

A group of followers who will stand for and submit to His headship.

A group of followers who will sit under the Lord Jesus Christ and esteem Him above all else.

A group of followers who will give themselves fully to Him and to one another.

A group of followers who are willing to "waste" their lives on Jesus … both individually and corporately.

The earth awaits such a group.

May our Lord have that which His soul longs for … a Bethany, here and now, in you and in me.

Will you pay the price to make that happen?

TALKING IT OVER

The following questions are designed for group discussion and interaction.

Chapter 1

1. Share a story about how a fellow Christian rejected you. What feelings did that create in you?

2. When the Lord was arrested, He was lied about, mocked, humiliated, assaulted, and then tortured to death by crucifixion. Reflect on how Jesus reacted to the people who did these things to Him when He rose again from the dead in comparison to how you or I would have been tempted to react.

3. Discuss all the times when Jesus was rejected when He was on earth, and reflect on how He understands your own rejections.

4. Discuss some of the ways that Jesus is still rejected today.

5. Why do you think brokenness is a neglected subject today among those who equip others for ministry?

6. Tell a story of how the Lord brought brokenness into your life.

Bitterness is like drinking poison and waiting for the other person to get sick. It hurts you, not them. If you are having trouble forgiving others, try this practical exercise, which may help you to release and forgive them.

*On a sheet of paper, write the names of every person who has hurt you. Leave five spaces below each name.

*Underneath each name, write what they did to you.

*When you are finished, raise the paper up to the Lord and tell Him out loud that you are releasing these people into His hands, forgiving what they did to you.

*Burn the piece of paper and thank the Lord for His release while you watch it turn to ash.

*If what they did to you comes back into your mind, tell the Lord that those people are His and you have released them.

Meet with your group after you have done this and share what the experience was like.

Chapter 2

1. When Lazarus shares his first encounter with Jesus in Bethany, what points stood out or touched you the most?
2. As far as your temperament goes, in what ways are you like Martha? In what ways are you like Mary?

3. The traditional caricatures of Mary and Martha are that Martha stood and served (not caring about worship) while Mary sat and soaked (not caring about service). In what ways does this chapter refute those two portraits?

4. If you used to be a Martha, share the story of what brought you to the place where you became a Mary.

5. What are some ways that we can sit at Jesus' feet and hear His word today?

6. In the "walking it out" section, three points were made about how to properly receive Jesus today. Which points spoke to you the most and why?

7. What are some of the things that make it difficult to live for an audience of One, and how can they be remedied?

Chapter 3

1. When Lazarus shares his second encounter with Jesus in Bethany, what points stood out or touched you the most?

2. Have you ever met a person who believed what one of Lazarus' three friends believed about sickness? If so, share the story.

3. What strikes you the most about John's narrative of Jesus raising Lazarus from the dead?

4. What do you think about the tears of Jesus? Can you add any further thoughts to what's been said about them in this chapter?

5. The gospel of John tells us that Lazarus was Jesus' friend. Make a list of the characteristics of what you consider to be a true friend.

6. Did Jesus fulfill all the expectations of a true friend that you listed for Lazarus? If yes, how? If not, how?

7. When Jesus heard that Lazarus was sick, He didn't act according to human need or expectation, but according to His Father's direction. Talk about the principle of Ishmael and Isaac in ministry and how this applies to how Jesus responded to Lazarus' sickness.

Chapter 4

1. When Lazarus shares his third encounter with Jesus in Bethany, what points stood out or touched you the most?

2. Describe how Mary may have felt when Judas and the other disciples rebuked her act of worship.

3. Have you ever had someone denigrate your worship or service to the Lord or regard it as waste? If so, tell the story.

4. Have you ever denigrated or second-guessed someone else's worship or service to the Lord? If so, how did you resolve it?

5. Have you ever been offended by another Christian? If so, how did you resolve it?

6. Have you ever done something to offend another Christian? If so, how did you resolve it?

7. To stir your affections for the Lord, try one or more of the following this week:

   *Take a nature walk and reflect on God's handiwork. Do nothing but observe and enjoy the Lord.

   *Make a list of all the things God has done to and for you and take a moment to give Him thanks for each one.

   *Listen to a Christ-centered message that reveals the glories of Jesus. ("Epic Jesus" is one example: http://frankviola.org/epicjesus). Afterward, spend some time quietly before the Lord, reflecting on what you heard.

   *Read Colossians 1 slowly out loud. When you are finished, turn the passage into a prayer.

   Meet with your group after you have done one or more of these things and share what your experience was like.

Chapter 5

1. When Lazarus shares his fourth encounter with Jesus in Bethany, what points stood out or touched you the most?

2. Why do you think Jesus chose Bethany as the place from which He ascended into heaven?

3. What are the practical implications of being raised with Christ?

4. What are the practical implications of being seated with Christ in heavenly places?

5. What are the practical implications of Jesus being our High Priest today?

6. Can you think of any other events that occurred on the Mount of Olives in the Gospels?

7. Do you think that Jesus will literally return to Bethany? Why or why not?

Chapter 6

1. When Lazarus ends his story about Jesus in Bethany, what points stood out or touched you the most?

2. Go back through the book and make a list of all the spiritual characteristics of Bethany.

3. Which of these characteristics have the most application for your life today? Explain why.

4. In what ways can you become more of a Bethany for your Lord?

5. In what ways can your church become more of a Bethany for your Lord?

6. Looking back on the narratives of Jesus in Bethany presented in this book, which ones were new to you?

7. What do you appreciate the most about Mary, Martha, and Lazarus?

NOTES

Facts about Bethany

1. John 11:3
2. John 11:5
3. John 11:11
4. John 11:36
5. John 11:38
6. Mark 14:5; John 12:5
7. John 11:1 KJV
8. John 11:18–19
9. Mark 14:3

Chapter 1: Appreciating Bethany

1. Luke 2:7 NLT
2. Matthew 2:16
3. John 1:11
4. Matthew 23:37
5. Luke 9:52–53
6. Mark 6:3–4
7. 2 Timothy 3:12
8. Matthew 23:37; Luke 19:41
9. Mark 15:10
10. Zechariah 13:6
11. Mark 14:41
12. John 15:20

13. Philippians 3:10

14. 2 Corinthians 1:5

15. Hebrews 4:15

16. 2 Corinthians 1:3–7

17. John 15:5

18. 2 Corinthians 12:9–10

19. 2 Corinthians 4:11–12

20. 2 Corinthians 4:7

21. Matthew 16:24–25

22. Luke 9:23; John 10:15; 13:37–38; 15:13; see also 1 John 3:16.

23. 1 Peter 2:21–23

24. Philippians 3:13

25. Philippians 2:13 KJV; see also Galatians 2:20.

Chapter 2: Awed in Bethany

1. I owe this insight to renowned New Testament scholar Craig Keener.

2. Proverbs 18:24

3. Luke 10:38 KJV

4. Matthew 10:40

5. Romans 15:7 NKJV

6. 1 Corinthians 12:21–23

7. 1 Corinthians 1:12–13

8. Colossians 3:11

9. Colossians 1:16, 18 NASB

10. Ephesians 3:16–17 NASB

11. Luke 10:40 NKJV

12. See Acts 22:3

13. See Luke 8:1–3

14. Luke 22:31

15. Acts 9:4

16. Matthew 23:37

17. Matthew 27:46

18. Luke 10:41–42 NKJV

19. Psalm 27:4

20. Philippians 3:13–14

21. Philippians 3:8

22. Psalm 127:1

23. Ephesians 1:20; 4:1; 6:11

24. Hebrews 4:10

25. Matthew 6:5

26. John 5:44

Chapter 3: Awakened in Bethany

1. John 11:3, 5, 11, 36

2. Ephesians 6:13–14 KJV

3. Romans 8:31

4. Hebrews 4:15 KJV

5. Luke 19:41

6. Hebrews 5:7

7. John 11:35

8. Hebrews 13:8

9. Proverbs 17:17

10. John 11:24, 27 NIV 2011

11. John 11:40

12. Matthew 16:16 KJV

13. John 10:40; 11:6

14. John 11:3, 5, 11, 36

15. John 11:41–42

16. See *Jesus: A Theography*, Leonard Sweet and Frank Viola (Nashville: Thomas Nelson, 2012).

17. 1 Corinthians 3:12
18. Romans 11:36
19. KJV
20. WE
21. ESV
22. Hebrews 2:15
23. Galatians 5:1
24. 2 Corinthians 3:17
25. Romans 6:18
26. Romans 8:21
27. John 8:36
28. Revelation 12:11
29. Luke 4:18–21
30. John 5:25
31. John 5:28
32. John 11:11
33. John 8:51
34. John 11:26
35. 1 Corinthians 15:56
36. John 11:11
37. Acts 7:60
38. 1 Corinthians 11:30
39. 1 Corinthians 15:20
40. 1 Thessalonians 4:13–14
41. 1 Thessalonians 5:10
42. ESV
43. John 11:21, author's paraphrase
44. 1 Peter 2:8 ESV
45. Matthew 11:3, author's paraphrase
46. Matthew 11:4–6, author's paraphrase
47. ESV

48. John 15:18

49. John 6:53–66

50. Isaiah 55:9

51. Romans 8:28

52. See John 6:26

53. Job 2:10 NLT

54. See Daniel 3:15.

55. See Daniel 3:16–18

56. Luke 14:26; Mark 10:28–30

57. Proverbs 3:5

58. Mark 7:37 ESV

59. Romans 11:33 KJV

60. John 11:11 GW

Chapter 4: Anointed in Bethany

1. John 12:9-11

2. Johnston M. Cheney and Stanley Ellisen, *The Greatest Story Ever Told* (Sisters, OR: Multnomah, 1994), 191–92.

3. 1 Corinthians 6:11 NLT

4. Ephesians 2:5 ESV

5. Luke 10:38–41

6. John 11:28–33

7. John 12:1–9

8. Matthew 20:1–15

9. 2 Corinthians 4:7

10. John 19:39 NASB

11. John 12:3

12. 2 Corinthians 2:14–15

13. Matthew 26:10

14. Deuteronomy 15:11

15. Matthew 2:11

16. John 12:3–5

17. Ephesians 1:17 KJV

18. Mark 11:1–10

19. Mark 11:11

20. Mark 11:14

21. Matthew 21:18–22, Mark 11:12–26, and Luke 19:45–46 from Cheney and Ellisen, *The Greatest Story Ever Told* (Sisters, OR: Multnomah, 1994), 194–195.

22. Mark 11:19; Matthew 21:17

23. Jeremiah 8:13; 29:15–19; Hosea 9:10, 16; Micah 7:1–4; Nahum 3:12

24. John 1:11 KJV

25. James 3:2

26. Genesis 50:20

27. 2 Samuel 16:11–12

28. Proverbs 16:28

29. Proverbs 6:16–19, author's paraphrase

30. Hebrews 12:15

31. Matthew 18:15

32. Proverbs 19:11

33. Mark 6:3

34. Matthew 25:40, author's paraphrase

35. Ephesians 4:26, author's paraphrase

36. James 1:19

37. Philippians 2:13

38. Compare John 2 with John 12.

39. Leonard Sweet and Frank Viola, *Jesus: A Theography* (Nashville: Thomas Nelson, 2012), 234–236. Used with permission.

Chapter 5: Ascended in Bethany

1. Romans 8:26–27, 34

2. 2 Corinthians 5:20

3. Philippians 1:8

4. Romans 6:2–6; 2 Corinthians 4:10; 5:14

5. 2 Corinthians 4:10–11; Colossians 1:24; Philippians 3:10

6. Romans 6:4; Colossians 2:12

7. Romans 6:4; Colossians 2:12–13; 3:1; Ephesians 2:6; Philippians 3:10

8. Ephesians 1:20–21; 2:6

9. Romans 8:30

10. Romans 5:17; Ephesians 1:20–21; 2:6

11. Hebrews 2:17

12. Hebrews 3:1

13. Hebrews 4:14

14. Hebrews 6:20

15. Hebrews 7:26

16. Hebrews 8:1

17. Mark 16:19

18. Hebrews 1:3

19. Colossians 3:1

20. Romans 8:34

21. Ephesians 1:20–23; 2:5–6

22. Matthew 28:18; Ephesians 1:22–23

23. Zechariah 14:4

24. For details on the Lord's second coming, see Sweet and Viola, *Jesus: A Theography*, chapter 16.

25. Revelation 21:1–3

Chapter 6: Anticipating Bethany

1. Hebrews 13:13 NLT

2. Mark 10:21, author's paraphrase

3. 1 Timothy 6:10

4. Genesis·1:2

5. Isaiah 66:1

ACKNOWLEDGMENTS

Kudos and heartfelt thanks to my friends Eric Wilson and Melissa Norris for strengthening the manuscript with their matchless eyes. Special gratitude to Joel B. Green, Craig Keener, Ben Witherington, J. C. Ryle, Alexander Moody Stuart, William MacCallum Clow, James Culross, John Macduff, Marcus Loane, G. Campbell Morgan, F. F. Bruce, Leon Morris, R. V. G. Tasker, Francis Moloney, Bruce Malina, N. T. Wright, T. Austin-Sparks, and Watchman Nee for some of the historical and textual insights. Warm thanks to a group of precious Christians I met in Owensboro, Kentucky in May 2012 where I delivered the messages upon which this book is based. The epigraphs in each of the chapters come from Ora Rowan's seminal hymn, "Hast Thou Heard Him, Seen Him, Known Him?"

"The book is finished. Let the writer play."

~Fifteenth-century monk

ABOUT THE AUTHOR

FRANK VIOLA has helped thousands of people around the world to deepen their relationship with Jesus Christ and enter into a more vibrant and authentic experience of church. He has written many books on these themes, including *From Eternity to Here*, *Revise Us Again*, *Reimagining Church*, *Finding Organic Church*, *Jesus: A Theography*, and *Jesus Manifesto*. His blog, *Beyond Evangelical* (frankviola.org), is rated as one of the most popular in Christian circles today.

LOOKING FOR MORE?

In September of 2013, Frank will be releasing an online course entitled "Learning How to Live by the Indwelling Life of Christ." This course will build on the lessons found in this book and make them practical. To see a sample of the course along with free resources for this book, go to GodsFavoritePlace.com.

BIBLE CREDITS

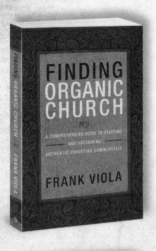
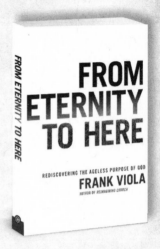
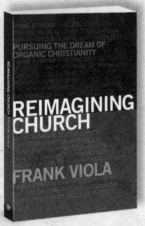